Has Anyone Seen My Reading Glasses?

To order additional copies, please contact us.
BookSurge, LLC
www.booksurge.com
1-866-308-6235
orders@booksurge.com

PAT PACIELLO

HAS ANYONE SEEN MY READING GLASSES?

The Humorous and Slightly
Informative Chronicles of a
Retired Baby Boomer

2006

Has Anyone Seen My Reading Glasses?

TABLE OF CONTENTS

If It Were Possible, I Would Like To Acknowledge Every Single Person In The Greater New York City Area. Let's Face It, If Your Name Was Mentioned In This Book You Would Definitely Purchase It, And I Would Have A Best Seller On My Hands. But Since This Is Not Practical, Let Me Thank Several Key People: First, Judy Nonemaker My "Editor," Who Worked Overtime To Correct My Faulty Grammar, And Served As My Sounding Board And Writing Coach; My Brother Tom Who Meticulously Reviewed My Book And Forced Me To Draft A Better Product; My Children Jay And Karin, Who Utilized Their Computer Knowledge To Help Make The Manuscript Presentable; And Lastly My Wife Ethel Who Not Only Permits Me, But Encourages Me To Continue My Peter Pan Retirement.

INTRODUCTION

It seems like yesterday when we Baby Boomers were in college mapping out our futures, and today we are closer to considering life changes than we are to moving up the corporate ladder. Nobody has really prepared us for this next phase in our lives. You did not learn about retirement planning in school, and when you were young, you would have laughed at an individual attempting to give you guidance on this subject. For some people, the first time that retirement surfaces is that fateful day right before you turn 50. You open an envelope that you presume is junk mail. You quickly scan the letter; eventually it registers. You have been invited to join AARP Foundation, (formerly The American Association of Retired Persons). The questions race through your brain. How can this be? It must be a mistake! They are confusing me with my father. I'm just a kid. How could I be a senior? I don't even consider myself an adult!

However, retirement is actually a very exciting time. You get the opportunity to do the things that you want to do rather than the things that you have to do (i.e., a job). Maybe you want to start a new business and become an entrepreneur, mentor disadvantaged children, write that novel that has been festering in your brain, or start an oldies rock band. Your choice is really only limited to your imagination.

As Baby Boomers, our retirement years are vastly different than that of our parents' generation. We enjoy a host of technological advances, many of which have both leisure time and business applications. Corporations are targeting Boomers to ensure our happiness and get a piece of our substantial economic pie. The opportunities that exist for us today were barely in the planning stages when our parents investigated retirement.

Being a new retiree, I went to the bookstores and logged on to the Internet to gain some insight on what I could expect in the future. I was disappointed to find out that the books that focused on the Baby Boomer generation treated the subject in a similar way. They broke down retirement into many different aspects, and supported their positions with a myriad of governmental statistics, polls, and surveys. The writers were not speaking from personal experience, and most of the books treated retirement in a somber fashion. "Beware of this!" "Don't end up penniless!" "Here is an example of a retirement gone sour!"

I may not be the smartest guy in the world, but being able to retire sooner rather than later should be a cause for celebration. If getting up in the morning without a mandatory agenda, free to do as you please, makes you uncomfortable, I suggest that you should consider therapy.

The first two chapters of this book outline my background prior to retirement. Besides revealing that the author's qualifications for writing this book are suspect, this pre-retirement section serves as the vehicle for the remainder of the book, which details my experiences and observations during the first five years of my retirement. Hopefully, you can identify with my journey and have a few laughs along the way.

CHAPTER 1
College

On April 7, 2000, I officially started the next phase of my life, retirement, at 50 years of age. I was not dependent on a weekly payroll check for the foreseeable future, and when I woke up in the morning I had no place to go and no agenda to follow. I had reached the middle class dream, or at least my dream—retire early while still young and healthy enough to enjoy the activities of youth.

I graduated college in 1972. I am quite sure I was the worst student to ever receive a degree in 4 years in the history of Fairleigh Dickinson University (a small Liberal Arts school in Teaneck, New Jersey). During my four years in college, the country was in the grip of the Vietnam War. The hippie movement, anti war protest, and civil disobedience were the order of the day. This chaotic, stormy period of history proved to be a godsend for me. Some professors believed that traditional grades A-F were arcane and they changed their grading system to pass/fail. Attendance was not mandatory and your grade would not be affected if you did not show up for a class. I thrived in this take-no-responsibility and no-accountability environment. I was a Psychology major. It was widely known that the psych curriculum was very easy and the professors were more likely to smoke pot with you and discuss the meaning of life than give you a failing grade. Plus, it didn't hurt that my fraternity had an extensive database of psychology term papers compiled over the years and made easily available to its members.

My friends and I were not politically active. As a matter of fact, the only demonstration I participated in was one to expand the gym facilities on campus. I was, however, very empathetic to any social protest that drew large numbers of co-eds, since these venues produced the best opportunities to meet girls. It took me exactly one semester to believe that college was a joke. By the second semester, I was missing as many classes as I was attending. The cafeteria was the focal point for our group and there was no way you could leave for class if you were losing money while playing poker. On the other hand, if you were fortunate enough to win a few hands, the other players insisted you give them a chance to win back their money. Drinking, drugs, and parties filled up most of our time, leaving very little for scholastics.

The first day of junior year, things started to spiral downward. A group of us partied all night long. A friend and I passed out in front of Becton Hall. We woke up at about 8:00 am hearing conversations that seemed to be coming from the sky. We had no idea where we were, nor how we got there. Students were walking over us to get to their classes. Once we came to our senses and our feet, we looked at each other in our dew-soaked clothes covered with grass stains and we laughed uncontrollably all the way to our cars before campus security arrived.

My scholastic career continued to deteriorate. I not only stopped attending my classes, but also no longer bothered to buy textbooks. Why waste the money, when the books would never be opened anyway? As a senior, I truly hit rock bottom. I lived in a fraternity house located in Palisades Park, New Jersey, that housed ten brothers and served as the focal point for our

40 members. The Frat House was a ratty place suffering from years of neglect and the abuse that only college boys could dole out. Two years after I graduated, the fraternity disbanded, and after an inspection by its new owner, the house was bulldozed to rubble.

The Brotherhood was made up of a diverse group. One half consisted of the stereotype hippies of the late 1960's. Long hair, peace symbols, tie-dyed tee shirts, and heavy drugs were the common theme for this group. Marijuana, cocaine, and most of the pharmaceuticals of the day were being consumed on a regular basis. The other half concentrated their efforts mostly on alcohol. Beer blasts, heavy drinking, and recreational drug use (marijuana) were the norm. This group wore their hair long hair by today's standards, but stopped just short of embracing the whole counterculture revolution. I was part of the latter group. The irony was that in 1968 as college freshmen we were all squeaky clean, All-American boys. Three, four years later we had gone through a major cultural facelift. The only question was how far we were going to take this ride and whether we could get back to reality when it ended.

It got to the point where I stopped going to campus, playing cards, and even participating in sports. I simply began sleeping my life away. During my last semester I rarely saw the sun. My routine was to go out and party with friends beginning at 10:00 pm. We would go clubbing in New York City and New Jersey. I would get back to the frat at 5:00 am. I was incredibly tired, drunk, and high. Since I had nothing to do the following day, I would sleep right through it. At 5:00 pm or so, I would wake up, make myself something to eat and prepare for the long night ahead. This routine continued for months. One day I was sleeping in my bed in the afternoon when I heard voices talking all around me. I was in that semiconscious state where you are not sure if you are dreaming or awake. I heard a familiar voice say, "Be quiet, and don't wake him up. It's true, man; the dude sleeps all day, every day. He is like a vampire." I opened my eyes and I was surrounded by a bunch of ZZ Top look-alikes observing me as if I were some kind of human lab experiment. They were friends of one of my hippie-freak brothers, who took them on a field trip to witness this human oddity. He apologized for waking me and invading my space, and his commune left quickly. In that instant, my life changed. Here was a group of people who were perpetually high and seldom coherent, and yet were looking at me as some sort of freak of nature. I had two choices: buy a white robe and start my own cult, or smell the roses, clean up my act, and rejoin the real world before it was too late.

For the first time in my college career I panicked. Somehow, I had managed to beat the educational system (or use the system) to earn 3.5 years of college credits. Now, with graduation less than a month away, I was on track to achieve a 0.00 grade point average for the semester. My grades would qualify me for membership in Delta House Fraternity, from one of the classic movies of all time, *Animal House*. My future seemed just as hopeless. It was time to go to work!

The psychology courses were a breeze. As I mentioned earlier, I tapped into our database of term papers and reconfigured an A paper into a solid B+. My electives were pass/fail. What teacher would deny you graduation because you failed Introduction to Golf and Basic Typing? I knew these courses would not be a problem. My concern was a political science course, *History of the World from 1917 to the present*. The professor was an old curmudgeon out of step with the culture of the late 60's and early 70's. He actually expected his students to come to class, study, do homework, and earn the appropriate grade in his class. What nerve! Unfortunately, he was not allowed to fail students for not showing up to class. His course was not pass/fail, but the traditional A-F grading system.

Every Tuesday and Thursday, the professor would have roll call before the start of his class. He was the only teacher to my knowledge that still took attendance at F.D.U. I had several of my fraternity brothers in that class. The teacher would start the roll call: "Costa?" "Here," "Ninger?" "Here," "Orlando?" "Present." "Paciello?" The silence was deafening. For every class a different friend or Frat Brother would raise his hand and say something like, "Pat is very sick," or "He's at the doctor's office and he might have pneumonia." By the end of the semester, I had contracted a new disease every Tuesday and Thursday, much to the delight of the students and to the chagrin of the professor. Imagine the teacher's surprise, when on the last class before finals, he took attendance and called out my name, "Paciello," and a sheepish voice in the background whispered, "Here." The professor lowered his reading glasses and peered out into the audience asking, "Who said that?" I raised my hand and he immediately told me to stand up. "What is your name?" he said. "Pat Paciello, sir." "Class, let us rejoice, there really is a Pat Paciello." The students howled, giving me a thunderous round of mock applause. My face turned flush as I shuffled my feet back and forth. When the applause ended, I timidly said to the professor, "May I speak to you after class, sir?" "Of course, Mr. Paciello." The sarcasm in his voice was dripping from his lips.

I had rehearsed my performance a number of times. My approach mirrored the Eddie Haskell character on the old T.V. show *Leave it to Beaver* (Eddie was obnoxiously sweet and polite to the Beaver's parents, but he was in reality mean and annoying to the Beaver). "Professor, thank you for giving me some of your time; I realize I have not been in your class for the entire semester, but please let me explain what transpired. I was raised in a very strict Catholic environment. When I went away to college the opportunities to explore a different life style and experiment with the changing culture overwhelmed me. I guess you could say I was a victim of sex, drugs, and rock and roll. I was befriended by people who took me down the wrong path and I dug a huge hole for myself. Only recently did I realize what a mistake I have made. If you can somehow give me an opportunity to pass your course, I promise I will reward your confidence."

I must say this was an Academy Award winning performance. As with most things in life, there was some truth blended in with a lot of fluff. I was sure I had hit a home run and the teacher would soon grab for his handkerchief to dry the tears from his eyes. Unfortunately, I was wrong. The professor was not buying my story. I had underestimated him.

The old-timer had seen and heard it all before. "Mr. Paciello, that is a very interesting story; however, my job is to teach the students in this class, and you have not been part of this class. You did not take the mid-term or the other quizzes, so at this point in the class, your grade is zero." My shoulders slumped. There would be no graduation. My parents would be devastated. They had put aside the money for my tuition, which was not an easy feat. They had no clue that I was a college student in name only.

The professor continued, "I am, however, a fair man. I'll tell you what, Mr. Paciello; the final is in ten days. I will give you the benefit of the doubt and give you a grade for this course based on the grade you get on the final." Translation, "I don't believe your story, but it is so outrageous that I will give you a chance to make a fool out of yourself and simultaneously clear my conscience." My eyes brightened. I thanked him profusely, sounding like a death row inmate who at the last minute had been pardoned by the governor.

I left the classroom feeling pretty good about myself. Now, I had to read a 1,200 page textbook, and retain all the information. But first I had to find the book! Not an easy task with only two weeks left till the end of the semester. It took me three whole days, but I finally bought the book from a student who used it the previous semester and had forgotten to sell it back to the bookstore. (The bookstore copies were long gone by the time I inquired about the textbook).

The next seven days were a blur to me. My only goal was to read and absorb the information in this massive history book. I barely slept and hardly ate. No Doze and amphetamines were my constant companions. I went from the happy-go-lucky quasi student who slept all day, to a cranky irritable student who never went to sleep. Finally, it was time to take the exam. I could barely keep my eyes open. When I completed the exam, I didn't know if I had scored a zero or a hundred, and at that moment I really didn't care. I just wanted to go to sleep.

One week later I was walking past Becton Hall when I spotted the professor walking straight towards me on a direct collision course. This was it. The moment of truth! I did my very best Eddie Haskel impersonation, "Hello, Professor. How are you?" I sounded so insincere; it actually startled me when the words came out of my mouth. The teacher did not respond, but motioned me to come over to one of the benches. I thought, "I am done. Not only did I fail the exam, but he is also going to rub it in my face." He opened his briefcase and pulled out a manila folder, obviously the graded exams. "Mr. Paciello," he bellowed as he quickly plucked my exam from the thick file, "I don't know how you did it, or what devious methods you employed, but out of 96 students who took my exam, you received the highest grade. However, I can assure you that I will investigate this matter and uncover the truth." I was stunned. I started to give my Oscar-winning acceptance speech, thanking him for giving me the opportunity, when he quickly jammed the exam book back into his briefcase, said "good day," and motored off as if the grim reaper were chasing him.

It took me all of two minutes to regain my sense of bravado. I was not only going to ace this class, but probably get the best grades since I had been in school. The system was a joke. One week later, I received my grades in the mail. I opened the envelope with great eagerness. As anticipated, I read off, "Pass, Pass, A, B, and finally my Political Science grade, a "C." How could this be?

I was hot; that S.O.B. screwed me. He couldn't bear to give me the grade I was entitled to. I yelled at my girlfriend, "I am going to the head of the department. This is outrageous!" My tirade continued with a volley of four letter words. Finally, my girlfriend interrupted, "Are you crazy? Leave well enough alone. Do you know how lucky you are to be graduating? You should have been thrown out of here three years ago." Quickly, I realized she was absolutely right. Here was a girl with looks, compassion, and common sense. Six months later, we were married.

CHAPTER 2
Working Stiff

As poor as my academic performance was, it was absolutely brilliant compared to my early adventures in the work force. After experiencing the academic world and sampling what working for a living was like, my fantasy was how I could put myself in a position not to rely on a job, yet have enough money to do the things that I wanted to do.

My first brush with employment came in October of 1964. I was the oldest son of three boys. My father was typical of "America's Greatest Generation." He worked two jobs while my mother stayed home and raised three kids. My father always wanted to know why I was not working either after school or during the summer months. This query started when I was nine and continued religiously every year.

One day, my dad came home with a big smile on his face. "Pat, I have a surprise for you. I got you your first job." Having no desire to work, I quickly responded, "Dad, I am only 14. You have to be at least 16 to get your working papers." "No problem," he replied. "The person doing the hiring owes me a favor and he assured me that you will be working." Insincerely, I muttered, "Great, where is the job?" "Yankee Stadium. You are going to be a vendor," he replied. My eyes widened. I lived in the shadow of Yankee Stadium and would often walk to the stadium after school and try to get the Yankees' autographs.

My friends and I would patrol the area in front of the players' entrance. We assumed that anybody driving a late model Cadillac must be a ball player. When the person emerged from his car, he was routinely greeted by thirty to fifty teenagers with paper and pencil in hand. Some were ball players and others were businessmen and Yankee stadium employees who happened to drive new cars. The ball player would usually give three to four autographs and then proceed inside the stadium. If you wanted an autograph, you had to be pretty crafty. Once you spotted a potential target, you had to proceed in a brisk walk. If you started running, the other autograph hounds would pick up the scent, and quickly turn into a frenzied mob. If someone was running to engage a player, that player must be a star, possibly Mickey Mantle, Yogi Berra, or Whitey Ford. We also used to go to the Concourse Plaza Hotel where the visiting team would stay. When you reached the hotel, you participated in a great game of cat and mouse, pitying the underage autograph seekers who were barred from the hotel by the veteran security force sworn to deny access to the players at all costs.

Back in the 60's, autographs had no financial value. You collected them as you would collect baseball cards, marbles, or bottle caps—for the fun of it. Like most of my generation I squandered, lost, and abused the Topps baseball cards that we collected in sets over many years. Vintage cards, which today would be worth a lot of money, were likely to be pinched inside your bicycle spokes for sound effects, flipped on the muddy sidewalks of the city, or traded in the school yard, which became the New York Stock Exchange for adolescents. The staccato cadence of the street brokers resonated throughout the neighborhood: "Got um, need um, got um, got um." You constantly made trades, yet nobody ever held on to the cards and they ultimately disappeared. Fortunately, at some point, we stopped chewing that rock hard pink piece of cardboard that Topps called gum. I truly believe that gum single-handedly spawned the dental industry in New York City. I have a theory that the owners of the baseball card companies were a conglomerate of dentists who needed a way for kids to purchase this cavity-producing product, and used the cards as a clever ploy to misdirect the consumer,…but enough with my conspiracy theories for now.

I had a number of older friends who worked as vendors in Yankee Stadium. This was a prize job. If you were sharp and willing to hustle, you could make excellent money. The guys I knew made more income on a Saturday or Sunday baseball game than friends who worked part-time after school for 5 days. Even better than that, you were inside Yankee Stadium watching your heroes play. You were a bit player in a sports drama that unfolded before your eyes. My first day on the job was the 5th game of the 1964 World Series. Future Hall of Famer Bob Gibson was scheduled to take the mound for St. Louis, versus Mel Stottlemyre, recently retired pitching coach of the Yankees. Even if I didn't make money as a rookie vendor, I was going to be at a World Series game. For a 14-year-old boy, this was a dream come true.

My father drove me to Yankee Stadium the following morning. We arrived at 6:00 am. He left for work and wished me good luck. Quickly, the area filled up with potential vendors. I recognized several of the older boys from the neighborhood. I immediately tagged along with them, as I had no clue what to expect or what I was supposed to do. Eventually, the supervisor appeared. He made a short speech, telling the prospective workers that less than half of the group would be working for the day and that if you had minimum experience, you basically had no shot. "Great," I thought to myself. "I have zero experience. I have been up since 5:00 and now I have to walk back home accomplishing nothing. Thanks, Dad!" The supervisor started to bark out names. If he called your name, you replied, "Here," and moved over to the side. As this exercise started to unfurl, I conjured up movie clips from *On the Waterfont* with Marlin Brando and Lee J. Cobb, the scene where the workers shape up on the docks hoping to be called for work. While I was daydreaming, I was startled to hear "Paciello" being broadcast from the coordinator. One of my friends gave me a sharp elbow to my side and in a falsetto voice, I squeaked, "Here." My friends congratulated me. They now proceeded to give me an orientation on policies and procedures and offered me tips and advice on how to succeed on my first day.

My friend Barry cautioned me, "Don't expect to make a lot of money on your first day. You are going to make mistakes, give out the wrong change, ruin some inventory, etc. We all earned less money the first time we worked, but by the second time we worked, everything was fine." I thanked him for the advice, but I was sure that I would not repeat the mistakes of my friends.

The vendors are assigned to different groups: beer, peanuts, hot dogs, etc. I was awarded souvenirs. A supervisor outfitted me with an apron and proceeded to fill my pouch with Yankee autographed baseballs. The other pockets were stuffed with glossy black and white player photos. World Series and Yankee pennants protruded from my back. I signed a receipt for the inventory that I received and waddled out of the supply room. I must have looked like a pregnant midget dressed as a piñata but I felt cool.

It was time to go to work. I followed my buddies around the stadium like a lap dog, observing them as they sold their products to the arriving fans. I picked out an area in the mezzanine section on the first base side and claimed it as my turf. I went up and down the aisles screaming, "Yankee souvenirs here!" This was not rocket science. A person wants a pennant, you give them a pennant. They pay you and you move on to the next customer. Of course, you have the occasional wise guys who scream out to you, "Yo, souvenirs." You quickly huff and puff up the stairs to their seats. When you arrive, they ask you to send the beer guy over and proceed to have a good laugh at your expense.

All in all, things were going well until about the 4th inning. I was standing on the mezzanine level when a father and son wanted a pennant. I reached behind me to pull out a flag, but the pennants were tangled. I yanked the pennants out, but in the process I lost my balance and tipped forward as a ball in my pouch began slipping out of my apron.

I lunged to retrieve the ball, but this only made matters worse as the rest of my autographed balls leaped out of my pocket like prisoners attempting a jailbreak. A dozen balls were now dancing down the steps from the mezzanine to the field level. I unstrapped my apron and made a mad dash to attempt to retrieve the balls. I managed to pick up some of them. Several fans came to my rescue and returned balls that had landed at their feet. I was completely flustered. I didn't know how many balls were missing. I proceeded up the stairs slowly, armed with the balls that I had recovered. I felt like a tightrope walker who knows one missed step will result in disaster.

I didn't want to make the same mistake twice and continue to provide comic relief for the fans in my section. As I moved closer to the mezzanine, I saw two kids rummaging through my apron, which contained the rest of my inventory. I screamed at them, "Get away from there!" They both had pennants in their hands, and upon hearing my voice they bolted from the scene. I was powerless to stop them. I had no idea how much inventory was missing. I was lost. I gathered up my souvenirs and half-heartedly continued to hawk my products.

Finally, the game ended and all of the vendors returned to the distribution point to return unsold inventory. It was now close to 6:00, which was a long workday for anyone, but especially for a 14 year old. The paymaster called out your name along with a dollar figure, "Jones, $97.20" or "Murray $114.73." The vendor would then pay that amount to the supervisor. Finally, my name was called, "Paciello, $72.80." Like the other vendors, I had counted my cash several times and I knew I only had $56.50. I gave the money to the cashier. He growled at me, "You are short $16.30. Where is the rest of the money?" "I don't have anymore money, Sir," I replied. "Well, you better get it, or you will be in a lot of trouble." I went to find my friend Barry who had just gotten paid. I explained what had just happened. He said, "You can't screw around with these guys. I will lend you the money, but you have to pay me back later." I thanked him, found the cashier, and paid my debt.

The cashier checked me off on his master sheet and continued calling the names of the other vendors. I just stood there for about ten minutes. Finally, I got up enough courage to ask the cashier, "When do I go to get paid?" He sarcastically replied, "You get the money that is left over." Perplexed, I said, "There is no extra money. I borrowed $16.30 from my friend Barry over there to pay you, and he wants his money back today. The cashier's face became rigid and his eyes bulged. He went into a 15 second diatribe outlining his opinion of me, using every four-letter word and guttural expression that I had ever heard.

I got the message and quickly left the stadium with Barry. We now had a long walk home. Barry answered my questions and tried to help me make sense of what had transpired on this bizarre day. Finally, I arrived back at my apartment. The door flung open and I was greeted by my dad with the words, "The bread winner is home."

The apartment was full. My uncle and aunt and my cousins were visiting. They were seated next to my two younger brothers and my mom. I pulled my dad over to the side and asked him for $16.30. He was puzzled. "Didn't you get paid?" I said, "Dad, please give me the money. I will explain later." He handed me the money, which I, in turn, gave to Barry.

Barry left immediately and now I proceeded into the living room where everyone was gathered. I felt like a Christian entering the Coliseum knowing his demise was imminent. I was immediately hit with a barrage of questions. Today was a big day for the family. The oldest son had become gainfully employed. My father beamed with pride. I had no choice. There was no escape. I timidly recounted what had transpired in the last 13 hours.

I waited for my father's reaction. He said, "Son, let me get this straight. I got you a job. You worked about 12 hours and it cost me $16.30. Is that about right?" I responded, "Sorry, Dad, but yes, that's true." "Well, thank God you didn't work for a week. I would have to go to the bank to take out a loan." He then started to laugh as hard as he has ever laughed, which broke up the audience in attendance. I felt like the village idiot, but I was surprised and appreciative that my dad saw the humor in my plight. I was determined to succeed as a vendor and erase the memory of my first experience, but there were no more home games in the World Series. I would have to wait for the first home game of the New York Giants football season to prove I wasn't a loser.

The football home opener finally arrived with great excitement and anticipation. As a sports fan, there is nothing better than the start of the professional football season. I was pumped up to root for my Giants and determined to make my second foray into the work force a big success. I arrived at Yankee Stadium much the same way as my first adventure. I was once again picked to work for the day. (Fortunately, for me, the ability to be chosen had nothing to do with prior performance.) I was no longer a rookie. I had paid my dues literally in more ways than one. I quickly walked to the supply room, eager to find out what I would be selling.

The answer came quickly. The supply master yelled out, "Paciello, hot chocolate." My friends, who were aware of my nightmare the first time I worked, formed a protective support group for me. They agreed that on a cold autumn afternoon, selling hot chocolate to the fans was a winner. (At least, nobody was going to run off with my tank of hot chocolate.)

I don't know how they make hot chocolate in the ballparks today, but in 1964, the process was quite an eye opener for me. The worker filled a large vat with the hottest water I have ever seen. The room was transformed into a huge steam bath. Milk was added, but it amounted to less than 1 quart for the entire vat! Then, the liquid substance was stirred with a giant piece of wood. Not a paddle or a mixing tool, but an old piece of wood, maybe a furniture leg. I watched in awe as the splinters from the wood swam down the river of hot chocolate. Two thoughts hit me immediately. One, I would never drink hot chocolate at a sporting event, and two, if the fans saw the manufacturing of the hot chocolate or for that matter how any of the food products were processed, they would rather starve than purchase anything to eat or drink at the stadium.

The hot chocolate was poured into the canister and hoisted onto my shoulders. I fell forward immediately from the weight on my back. The supervisor came over to me quickly, "If you can't carry the hot chocolate, give it to one of the older boys and you can sell souvenirs. "Souvenirs," I thought to myself, "no way." "I will be fine. Just slipped a bit," I replied. I was ready to make my fortune. I waddled out of the supply room a cross between Quasimodo and a dwarfed tin man.

I went straight to the expensive box seats on field level, eyeballing my first customer of the day. A mature—make that a very mature—woman waved at me. I lumbered forward. The woman was decked out more for a presidential inaugural than for a football game. She had on a floor length mink coat with a matching hat and sparkling jewelry on her hands and neck. I remember thinking, "What a waste of a football ticket." "Young man," she said, "I want a cup of hot chocolate. Is the hot chocolate hot?" "Yes, mam," I replied, "I can assure you, it is hot." She persisted, "Well, if it is not hot, then I am not going to pay you for it."

I reached out for the cup dispenser on the side of my tank. To my dismay, my short arms could barely reach across my body and I had to hold the cup with my left hand, while I poured the hot chocolate from the spigot with my right hand. As the cup filled up, I could not believe the heat that was searing my fingers. My hand felt like it was on fire. "How can this hurt so much," I thought.

Finally, I couldn't take the pain any longer and I tossed the cup away from me. Unfortunately, the molten liquid found its way to the mink coat worn by my customer. She went absolutely crazy. "You ruined my mink coat. You are going to pay for a new coat. Where is your supervisor?"

Everything was a blur to me. My hand was still throbbing. The woman was screaming at me and I pictured myself returning home from work, telling my dad that I needed $5,000 or I was going to jail. I tried to regain my composure. "Don't worry, ma'am, I am going to get a supervisor." She turned her back to clean off the coat and I seized the moment. I ran as hard and fast as a little kid can, with a small silo strapped on to my shoulders. I never looked back.

I went to the opposite side of the stadium to the top of the grandstand. My left hand was actually beginning to form blisters. I stared at the cup. It was a wax-coated soda cup, not a Styrofoam hot chocolate cup. I was going to have to run away from home to avoid the embarrassment and humiliation created by my actions, all because some supply worker outfitted me with the wrong cups!

I was tired, dejected and scared. I thought the police were on a manhunt searching for me throughout Yankee Stadium. I imagined Bob Sheppard, the voice of Yankee Stadium (he still mans the P.A. system at the Stadium today) interrupting the game and in his distinctive voice saying, "Excuse me, ladies and gentlemen, the security staff and NY Police are looking for a 14 year old boy masquerading as a vendor selling hot chocolate. If you see him, do not try to apprehend him, as he is armed and dangerous. Please notify the nearest stadium personnel. Thank you." I unhooked the hot chocolate, sat down on the floor, and proceeded to cry.

One of my friends, who was selling hot dogs eyeballed me and made a beeline towards me. "Pat, what's the matter? Did you get hurt?" I rubbed my swollen eyes; embarrassed that one of the older guys knew that I was crying. I told him my plight and what had just occurred. He smiled at me. "This isn't the end of the world. Nobody's going to arrest you. You stick with me and follow me around. We will be a team. I will sell the fans a hot dog and you provide the hot chocolate. We will have fun and you will make money. You'll see." I rose up somewhat reluctantly, but figured this was the best offer I was going to receive. As we walked down the aisles, my friend stopped and started to laugh. He said, "Kid, I can't believe you chucked hot chocolate on that old lady's mink. The look on her face must have been priceless. The next time you attack a customer, let me know in advance. I have to be there!" I looked at him and I started to laugh and off we went.

My friend was right. I sold plenty of hot chocolate and really had a good time doing it. My mentor made sure I didn't commit any gaffs. The game ended and it was time once again to "cash in" and get paid. My name was called and unbelievably once again I was short the amount of money that was required. I knew what this meant and proceeded to bang my head against some metal lockers cursing like a sailor and thinking, "I must be the stupidest person in the world. My picture is in the dictionary next to the word loser!" My mentor figured out what had happened and asked me which cashier had told me that I was short. I pointed him out. He said, "That figures. That bastard has done this before to new kids. He dummies up the total and he pockets your commissions and the money you owe for the shortfall." He approached the cashier with two other vendors that I knew. After several minutes of many threats and hyphenated words, the cashier called me over. "It looks like I made a mistake. It wasn't on purpose, but you get back $19.45. Now, get lost." I thanked my friends for their help and proceeded home. I was confident of two things. My dad would be proud of me, and I would never work at Yankee Stadium again.

Obviously, my first working experience as a youth was a disaster, but my father was a highly motivated taskmaster. He always worked two jobs, so the notion that his oldest son did not have even a part time job did not sit well with him. He was my personal "Headhunter" throughout high school and college. He made sure that I was working when I wasn't in school. I tried to counter his zealousness by proclaiming that I was a victim of A.L.S. (Acute Laziness Syndrome), but he had no sympathy for my disease. During my school years, my dad must have gotten me ten to twelve summer and part-time jobs. I was either fired from these jobs, or as a courtesy to my dad was kept to the end of the assignment on the condition that I never return.

Of all the employment fiascos, two experiences shine the brightest. I was a high school student working as a maintenance person for a residential condominium community in Yonkers, New York. I reported to a large German fellow named Fritz. He was the gardener/maintenance supervisor/Jack-of-all-trades. He had been working on the site forever and was none too happy to break in a high school student who would only be there for the summer. Fritz could best be described as a gruff, grouchy old man. He spoke with a thick German accent when he spoke to me at all. Most of the time, he grunted and made charade-like gestures to communicate with me. After being in his employ for two hours, he gave me my first assignment.

Fritz handed me a pair of hedge clippers, and told me to trim a row of hedges. He said he would be back in a half hour and limped away. I had the clippers in my hand with no idea what to do. I lived in the Bronx. We had no shrubs or grass, and if you needed maintenance in your apartment, you banged on the pipes. The super appeared, and he solved all of your problems. I did the best I could, but when Fritz returned he looked at my work and started to spew a variety of what I must assume was German profanity. His face was beet red and I thought he was going to have a heart attack. I retreated backwards to get a better perspective of my work and also to create some space between Fritz and myself. Even I was horrified. It looked like Edward Scissorhands on drugs had intentionally mutilated the property.

I apologized and tried to play the inexperience card with Fritz. He stormed off to the tool shed and barked at me to come along. After dressing me down and explaining how I had caused him extra work and potential trouble with the head of the condominium association, he told me to remain in the tool shed and not to touch anything. He had to fix a leaky pipe in one of the units and would be back in less than an hour.

As he was leaving, he pointed to one of the lawn mowers and said, "Oil the wheels, but don't do anything else." He pointed to the oil can and left. I knew immediately I was in trouble. I had never used a lawn mower before and obviously had never oiled one. I wanted to call out to Fritz who was disappearing from sight, but after the hedge incident, that was not an option. I looked at the mower.

I looked at the oil can. Unfortunately, they didn't move. I was hoping that the two main characters in this little play would find each other and get me off the hook…no such luck! I walked around the mower, checking and rechecking, looking for what must be a logical solution. I was sweating and time was growing short. Fritz asked me to do one simple assignment and I could not complete it. I looked out the window of the shed and saw Fritz advancing. "Hell, Pat. Do something. Even if you do the wrong thing, it's better than doing nothing!" I quickly finished my assignment and waited for Fritz to enter.

"You oil da mower?" he inquired. "Yes," I replied as I pointed to the machine. He peered down at the lawn mower and then did something I didn't think he was capable of. He started to laugh. More accurately, he started to laugh uncontrollably. He grasped his formidable beer belly with both hands and practically fell to the floor. He motioned to two other maintenance workers to come into the shed. In between seizure-like movements, he blurted out my assignment to them. His eyes were now flooded with tears from excess hilarity. Quickly the other workers joined him in this spontaneous laugh fest.

Upon seeing three grown men yuck it up, I started laughing even though I was the butt of the joke. What had I done to ignite these three people? I had simply taken the oil, and very neatly applied it to the rubber of the four tires! Now, I still don't know how to oil a machine, but I learned a valuable lesson that a lawn mower will not operate more efficiently if the tires are lubricated with oil.

My favorite, or should I say most infamous temporary work experience occurred when I was enrolled in college. I landed a summer position at the Scarsdale Country Club, a private haven for the well-heeled in Westchester County. If you remember "Bushwood" from the movie *Caddyshack,* you have a pretty clear picture of what Scarsdale Country Club was like. I was part of a crew that was responsible for the maintenance of the golf course. I would sweep the dew off the greens in the early mornings using a huge bamboo pole, cut grass, pick up leaves, debris, etc. It was a mindless job that paid well and offered little opportunity for me to screw up.

I was introduced to my fellow workers on my first day of employment. They were full-time, experienced, and were very competent in their jobs. Unfortunately for me, only one person spoke English and I didn't speak any Spanish other than a half dozen slang expressions that were part of every N.Y.C. schoolboy's vocabulary.

Initially, the crew was not too happy with me when they realized my level of incompetence, plus the fact that as a union employee my wages were equal to theirs. Quickly, however, I gained their confidence and friendship; For the most part, our communications consisted of pantomime and broken English, versus broken Spanish. Every day was like playing "Password" in a foreign language. When I would finally understand what they were trying to communicate to me, it was like winning on a quiz show. Unfortunately, there were no prize winnings, only the realization that I had to empty the garbage cans.

My new compadres opened up a different world to me. They were fun-loving and often child-like. One of their diversions during the workday was to try and capture rabbits that roamed the golf course. No easy task! Once the rabbits were caught, they were put into a large cage where they were diligently cared for. The key was to put a male and a female in the same cage. You talk about sex education! These rabbits put on a show that held everyone's attention, and the show seemingly never ended. You may hear about a guy who "does it like a rabbit"—No way! I don't care if he swallowed a vat of Viagra and was having sex with Pamela Anderson, Raquel Welch, or Marilyn Monroe, or all three at the same time. The lion may be King of the Jungle, but the rabbit was the king of Scarsdale Country Club.

During this time frame, I became good friends with a co-worker named Roberto. He was the only person in the crew who was about my age. Like the others, he was born in Puerto Rico. Roberto had only moved to the New York area recently and initially was very cool towards me. (I think he thought I was a government agent working for the Internal Revenue Service.) Once he realized that I was an incompetent goof-off we became fast friends. To make our workday more fun, we would compete and bet each other on all sorts of silly things. Who would win a 50-yard dash pushing a lawn mower? Who could hit a golf ball furthest into the woods? How many times would the rabbits have sex during our lunch break?

One day Roberto and I were assigned to pick up all the branches and tree limbs that had fallen on the ground from the previous night's storm. We had the rare opportunity to drive mini—trucks that included a cargo carrier that would store the debris we had accumulated. These trucks looked like your little red wagons from your childhood days pumped up on steroids. They utilized hand-held brakes and probably were built to go no more than 20 miles per hour. Roberto and I climbed into our trucks and proceeded to gather the loose brush.

Halfway through our assignment, he drove over to me and wanted to play a game of chicken. We were about 100 yards from a cliff that looked down upon a pond that guarded a small green on a Par 3 hole. The first person to stop his truck before the end of the cliff was the loser. You had to go full speed and could not touch the brakes until you were committed to stop.

I accepted his challenge immediately and called him every Spanish curse word that I could think of (and by now; I had developed a considerable vocabulary). He fired back in his feeble English and I could see that he was making great strides with four-letter and hyphenated words. We laughed at each other. I was determined to win this bet.

We took off and raced down a slight incline towards the cliff. The two carts were side by side. As the cliff grew closer, I would look at Roberto and he at me, hoping that the other would apply the brake and end this insanity. With the throttle at full and speeding down hill, it felt like the cart was going 120 mph. Of course, in reality it was going much less.

I heard Roberto scream, "No mas!" I immediately applied the hand brakes. Unfortunately, the vehicle was going so fast that the entire steering column ejected from the frame. Now I was holding the hand brakes, but nothing was connected to the truck.

What happened next is straight from a Roadrunner cartoon. Both vehicles flew off the cliff and plummeted into the pond. As the sportscaster Warner Wolf would say when he showed a NASCAR pile up or a horse racing collision, "Amazingly, nobody got hurt." I got thrown out of the truck. I was a little dazed and bruised and saw Roberto a few yards away flapping his arms uncontrollably. He saw me and grabbed on for dear life. I started laughing because it was apparent he didn't know how to swim. I tried to calm him down and demonstrate that I was standing and the water was less than 5 feet deep.

The members on the tee box looked at us with complete disdain. What audacity we must have, to interfere with their golf game. While Roberto and I regained our senses, a member barked at us, "Quiet. Man on the tee." Four tee shots were launched over our heads into the direction of the green.

Word quickly spread throughout the country club about what had transpired. Roberto and I knew we were in deep trouble. The golf course superintendent was off the premises. One of his assistants got his hands on a crane and proceeded to raise the trucks from the pond, as the members looked on. Play had been halted, and just when the truck attached to the crane was at its apex, here comes Woody, the superintendent, driving his Jeep across the golf course at warp speed. He looked up at the suspended truck. The veins in his neck were ready to explode. His jaw was clenched tight and he had a gaze that sent a chill up my spine. "Pat, come over here," he bellowed. He pulled me over to the side and demanded to know which one of these bleepety beeps bleepety beeps was responsible for this travesty. "Not only will that person get fired, but I'm personally going to beat the crap out of him." The more venom he spewed, the more I shrunk emotionally. I thought briefly about giving up Roberto, but this was his livelihood. For me, it was spending money for college. In a soft cracked voice, I responded, "It was my fault, Woody." He looked at me at first with shock, and then anger. He started to raise his hands. I thought he was going to choke me, but he paused, stormed back into the Jeep, and took off.

The next day Woody asked me to come into his office. He explained that for a sharp kid like me, this environment was a waste of my time. I agreed whole-heartedly and was gone within an hour. Eventually, and mercifully, my summer employment days were coming to an end. It was time to enter the real world and start looking for a permanent job. Babies clinging to their mother's womb at birth demonstrated more enthusiasm for the future than I did.

After graduation, I started my career in the employment staffing business working for an employment agency as a recruiter for the computer industry. My parents were horrified when I told them that I was making $100 per week as a base salary. "We paid your tuition for four years so that you could earn a good living as a professional and now you earn less than a high school graduate and you're called a head hunter?" They felt a little better when I told them that the trainees working for the firm without college degrees were only getting paid $90 per week.

My goal for my new career opportunity was a simple one,—avoid being fired for 16 weeks, (you needed to work 16 weeks to become eligible for unemployment insurance), get laid off, and then hop in my 1964 Volkswagen Beetle and drive cross-country with a friend and see America. I wasn't very confident that I could achieve this lofty goal. My previous work history, already documented in this book, gave no clue that my unblemished streak of futility was about to change. Fortunately, I had two things going for me. My best assets were my verbal skills and a high likeability factor, assets that were most prized and necessary for success in the recruiting business. The other factor was that the company was paying you so poorly that if you had a pulse and had not committed any capital crimes in the last 6 months they were profiting by having you in their employ. It was difficult to get fired, and for the first time, I didn't.

I moved up the ranks quickly at Wells Management Corporation, and after 7 years I was ready to start my own data processing staffing organization. I discussed the possibility of a partnership with a good friend, Anthony Destro, who like me, managed one of the most profitable offices for the company which employed us. Our timing proved to be impeccable. The computer industry was growing into adulthood and my current company was positioning itself to be acquired by a global staffing firm. The firm that I worked for was very profitable and immediately went into an austerity mode to make its bottom line more attractive to the new buyer. They started to freeze salaries and restrict earnings potential. Never a smart move, but for a sales organization it was a death knell. The result was a bonanza for Tony and me. We had the best and brightest employees eagerly wanting to contribute to the new organization that was about to be formed.

Tony and I built a very successful staffing organization over the next ten years with offices throughout New Jersey. The demand for the Information Technology professionals we represented outstripped the supply, which was the perfect ratio for talented recruiters. Of course, when your business sector is red hot, you credit market conditions for 10% of your success and the other 90% to your innovative management style and ability to execute your mission statement.

Having Tony as a partner was a unique experience. Not only was he a shrewd businessman and outstanding motivator, but also he was and is one of the foremost Elvis Presley impersonators in the country. Picture Elvis Presley wearing a three-piece suit, complete with black pompadour hairstyle, mutton chop side burns, laser Elvis belt buckle, and more jewelry than a rap star, and you have my partner. Tony's look opened eyes everywhere he went, but my favorite Tony story occurred in our first year of business with our new company. We were trying to put together a benefit package for our employees. We wanted to establish a 401K program and a company sponsored profit sharing plan. I contacted a large New Jersey bank whose trust department had a fine reputation. Tony and I were ushered into a large conference room—make that a corporate boardroom—surrounded by thick mahogany walls, Victorian chairs, and magnificent old paintings that signaled an era long since passed. The head of the trust department and his assistant entered the room. They were both distinguished men probably in their mid 60's who evoked an image somewhere between Alfred the Butler of the Batman television show fame and John Houseman, the actor and pitchman for Smith Barney, who uttered the famous advertising slogan, "We make money the old fashioned way. We earn it."

Immediately I realized that I had made a mistake. The bankers had not been alerted to the fact that one of the principals of the firm with which they were meeting was an Elvis Presley clone. We made the usual introductions, shook hands, and were presented with information packets. I looked up at the two bankers. They both seemed to be in a state of shock. Their brains must have been going into over-drive. If I were a mind reader, I'm sure their self-conversation went something like this, "Are you kidding me? Is this a joke? Who is playing a prank on me? Elvis is alive! But, why does he need a corporate benefit plan?" The two men never regained their composure. They tried not to be obvious, but they eyeballed Tony the entire meeting, probably expecting him to jump up and start singing "Viva, Las Vegas."

They made a half-hearted disjointed presentation of the bank's products. On the other hand, their fascination and enthusiasm for Tony was endless. They asked him a million questions. By the time the meeting had concluded, they had learned far more information about Elvis Presley than Tony and I had uncovered about their profit sharing and 401K plans. During the drive back to our office, Tony, who didn't fully appreciate how he turned these two staid businessmen into Elvis groupies, said he was unimpressed with their presentation. I smiled and nodded in agreement.

The 1980's were kind to most people in the business world. Tony and I were no exceptions. In the mid 80's, I started to think about retirement seriously for the first time. If we could continue this level of success to the end of the decade, I calculated that I could retire at 40 years old. By selling my half of the business, combined with money from savings and retirement investment plans, I could walk away from the staffing business and live a life of leisure or move into a new entrepreneurial setting. I almost made it! But, in the late 80's, the economy began to decline. Tony and I had too many offices staffed with too many employees who were competing for a dwindling market. We were slow to react. Thinking this downturn was a temporary blip on the staffing screen, we poured good money after bad into our operation. By 1990, we parted ways, closed the company, and moved in separate directions. Very quickly, retirement became a faded memory. Earning a living to support my family became my new priority.

The next two years were financial disasters. I started a new staffing firm and hired high-profile recruiting professionals. I learned a very simple economic lesson. If there is no demand for your product or service, and the supply of your product or service (i.e., Information Technology professionals) is great, you either change your business model or starve. Many friends and neighbors were laid off during this economic downturn. I, on the other hand, was the envy of my neighborhood. I owned my own company, set my own hours, and drove a nice car. Unfortunately for me, every day I worked, I lost money. (Payroll and expenses far exceeded revenue.) I was feeding a corporate monster whose appetite could not be satisfied. When was the market going to turn around? Was I an idiot to hold on, or would my "stay the course" resolve be rewarded? My empty checkbook and expanding debt made the decision for me. Stay in the game. Hang in there, but strip the business to the bone.

In 1993, the business climate was prepared to start its dramatic climb that would continue for the rest of the decade. I had a small staffing firm that was finally starting to run in the black, when a former employee, John Bottiglieri (no, not everyone in this book is Italian, it just seems that way), proposed reengineering the company to an information technology-consulting firm. We would provide talented computer professionals, put them on our payroll and lease them out to our corporate clients. Our internal staff would be expanded and retrained. I set up a pilot project and told John that if we made our projections, we would form a new company as equal partners.

Timing for the new venture could not have been better. Our clients could not snap up our consultants fast enough. The business was easy and very profitable. If your company had anything to do with computer technology, your chance for success increased dramatically. As usual, we were living in a false sense of reality, a reality that would lead to one of the harshest economic downturns in recent memory.

Business was so surreal that the mergers and acquisitions brokers started contacting us to act as an agent, to sell our business to large publicly held staffing firms. Our new business was less than two years old. This was madness. But when you are the commodity in this bizarro world, I say, "Bring on the madness!"

I thought about the successful business I had with my former partner, Tony, and how at the end it was worthless. I was getting a second chance to ring the bell and retire early. I entered into serious discussions with RCM Technologies, a public company who like their peers was gobbling up smaller consulting firms like little kids unleashed in a candy store. The more these publicly owned firms acquired new companies, the bigger they became, the better their balance sheets looked, and ultimately the stock price rose. Wall Street supported this house of cards strategy, assuming that any acquisition was a good acquisition, disregarding sound management and accounting principles.

I told RCM what John and I were looking to receive from them for the sale of the business. If they met the number, I would put the keys on the desk, and like Motel 6, leave the light on. To my surprise, they agreed. Well, almost. Both sides were in accord with the financial terms of the deal, but there was one caveat. John and I had to sign an employment contract for three years to manage our former company. To maximize the profits from the sale of the company, we had all kinds of bonus and incentive clauses built into the agreement. Failure to achieve certain benchmarks of profit margin would result in a reduced payout for the sale of our company. I put the golf clubs back in the closet, returned my Hawaiian shirts, and traded my flip-flops for wingtips. If all went according to Hoyle, in three years I would turn 50 and have the opportunity to investigate retirement and decide what I wanted to do with the rest of my life.

The three years with RCM proved to be eventful for me. It was my first experience working for someone other than myself since I had started as a trainee with Wells Management Corporation in the seventies. This new experience reaffirmed why I had developed my own business in the past. On one hand, RCM was very clever. Our office performed very well over the three years. RCM basically paid John and me for our company out of the profits we were generating for the three-year period. They were happy to pay us our performance bonuses, as it represented only a small percentage of the overall profit. They lived up to their financial agreement and both parties eventually received contractually what had been agreed upon.

However, the culture and management style was like oil and water to the bulk of new acquisitions including myself. RCM wanted to run its business like a Fortune 500 Company. Unfortunately, the organization was made up of dozens of small divergent firms, led by independent business owners whose sales mantra was to meet and exceed the profit quotas, receive their money and move on. RCM continued gobbling up other staffing companies. They purchased two firms 15 minutes from my office, all competing for the same business, all using the RCM name. In a word it was a mess—meetings, threats, and lawsuits were the order of the day.

I realized this situation was hopeless. I petitioned management to let me out of my contract early. They rejected my offer several times. One day, out of the blue, they called up and were eager to agree to my terms. They finally realized that they would be better off without this pain in the ass. They would terminate the contract six months earlier than stipulated. In two weeks, I would be off payroll and all aspects of the employment contract would be enforced. I was not permitted to work in the staffing business within a 100-mile radius for a period of 2 years. The paperwork was signed, handshakes extended, and I left the office for the last time. My goal of early retirement was realized and I didn't have a clue what the future held.

CHAPTER 3
The Second Beginning

The next day I awoke at the usual time, around 7:30, and I went downstairs. My wife was up and about cooking breakfast and getting the house in order. Today was a rare day off for her. She was and is a substitute teacher, secretary and school aid in our district. The school kids were off for Easter vacation. Ironically, her usual routine was being suspended at the same time that my retirement was beginning. "Well, does a retired man want breakfast?" she queried. Sure, pancakes would be great," I responded.

We ate breakfast and small-talked about how yesterday's day went at school. She asked me about my last day at work. We chatted about our three children. The oldest is working in the business world. The other two are students attending Penn State University. In about 45 minutes we covered every possible topic that we had in common. I glanced at my watch. It was almost 8:30 in the morning and I could not think of single subject with which to engage my wife in conversation. Finally, to break the awkward silence, I asked my wife what time we would be having lunch and whether she had a preprinted menu that I could study. She started to laugh. "You'd better get a new job real soon or we're both going to go crazy." It wasn't even lunchtime on my first day in retirement and my wife was reading me the riot act.

I then went into the family room and went to the holiest

of holy places, the couch. I get choked up writing about my couch. The couch is unquestionably man's best friend; combine that with a large-screen television and a remote and you have nirvana. There have been numerous couch thefts in my neighborhood, but due to my ability to meld with the couch as one for long hours at a time, my couch has never been stolen! I performed my usual ritual on the couch gathering the appropriate number of pillows and wrapping myself up with two blankets. I grabbed the remote and switched on ESPN. In a nanosecond, my wife yelled from the kitchen, "Are you crazy? We are not watching sports. There are three episodes of *Mash* running in a row today, and I never get to watch the program because I am working." My wife loves the old television show *Mash*, as much as I love the couch. I jumped on the computer for the next hour and a half and listened to my wife laugh at the old episodes—episodes she has seen in the past a dozen times. I figured this is a small price to pay. How shallow can I be? My poor wife works every day, and I don't even earn a living. Let her have her fun. In a week she will be back to work, and I once again can become king of my castle.

This progressive attitude of mine lasted less than 24 hours. The next day in the afternoon, *Mash* once again reared its ugly head, playing three episodes in a row. My wife was ecstatic. The only surprise was that these three episodes in the afternoon were the same episodes broadcast the prior morning. I guess you could say this was a rerun of reruns. I alerted my wife to this obvious folly. She answered succinctly, "Who cares?" and preceded to laugh at the same jokes she had heard only the day before. Was I in *Mash* hell, or an unwitting victim in a *Twilight Zone* episode? Was this going to be my reward for early retirement? It was obvious that I had two choices—one was to return to the workforce. I dismissed that option immediately.

The second was to convince my wife that she was cheating society by only having one job when so many people could benefit from her many talents and skills. I was making some serious progress when even I must admit, I went over the line. I cut out an advertisement for UPS. They were looking for workers to load their trucks on third shift 12 midnight to 8 am. I explained to my wife that sleep is so overrated and that the physical nature of the job would be akin to an intensive workout. Plus, the extra income she earned would give her a measure of independence and self-sufficiency that was her right. Fortunately, the soda can she threw at me missed. After hours of pleading, "I was only kidding," she accepted my apology. She asked if I could turn on the television because *Mash* was on. I added the two magic words that can save any relationship... "Yes, dear."

The first weeks and months of your retirement are a pivotal time. If you have not done the proper planning, and you are not sure that your spouse is on the same page, your retirement could become your purgatory. The role of your spouse cannot be underestimated in your retirement planning. Will both husband and wife be retired simultaneously? If this is the case, will you be doing the bulk of your activities together—golf, tennis, traveling, shopping, dancing, etc? Or do you have divergent interests? You want to play golf at the club followed by game of poker with the boys, while your wife, the more mature one of the relationship, does volunteer and charity work during the day. Will you be working part-time, while your wife stays home? Maybe your wife wants to continue with her career, while you remain unemployed. The point is, you have been programmed for most of your life. Everyone knows his or her role in the family. You left for work at 7:30 a.m. Monday through Friday. Your wife had her routine and the children went off to school. You rushed to go to soccer games, dance recitals, and so on. For many years you followed a fairly rigid schedule that didn't allow a lot of free time, and while you moaned about this hectic schedule, the truth is that you loved it! Things are different now. You have a blank canvas and you're free to paint any picture that you want. On the surface this seems easy—a slam-dunk, a home run and it may be, but now you have to make lifestyle decisions that will impact you and your spouse. The two of you have to be on the same page or your home run will turn into a strikeout.

As I mentioned previously, I quickly learned that my wife and I both being at home could be a recipe for disaster. She has her rituals and I was in her space. She eats a substantial breakfast and loves her java. I rarely eat breakfast and don't drink coffee. The first thing my wife does when she goes downstairs in the morning is to turn the television on. I watch way too much television, so I try not to turn on the tube until late in the afternoon. I love to watch movies on television uninterrupted from start to finish. My wife has too much nervous energy to sit still for two hours. These and many other lifestyle differences have always been part of our makeup, but in the past our two worlds wouldn't intersect and collide.

During my first days as a retired husband these lifestyle differences could not have been more apparent. My wife believes that electricity is a luxury, not a necessity. I support her position as long as I am not home and not being forced to live in the dark. I admit I am guilty of leaving the lights on in a room, and having the computer on for short periods when I am not utilizing it. However, my wife would come racing into a room that I had just vacated and immediately switch the lights off even though I was returning in a nanosecond. I was afraid to go to the bathroom, fearing that I would be plunged into a world of darkness when I opened the door. In fairness to my wife, I have my own peccadilloes. I have a penchant for opening closet doors and not closing them when I am finished. When you are working and not home during the day this faux pas is not a big deal, but when you are both home at the same time it becomes a problem. Out of frustration, Ethel placed stick-it reminders on key closets, the ones that held the food, alcohol, and sporting goods. She issued a warning and outlined the severe penalty for future violations. To no one's surprise, I not only continued to leave the closet doors open, but it took me three days to realize that the warning stickers existed.

My wife views heating a house as an evil that must be destroyed. When people are cold in their house they turn up the thermostat. My wife tapes the thermostat so that it can't be tampered with. The colder it gets; the more sweatshirts and blankets she provides. I wrap myself in so many articles of clothing that unless the cordless phone is within three feet, I have no chance answering the phone before the answering machine kicks in. When company visits, they think we are freezing meat somewhere in the house. On the other hand, our home is germ free. No microbe is brave enough to live in this environment. When I first retired, I tried to make my case for a frost-free home to my wife. I said, "This is ridiculous! I can afford to retire from my career at a young age, but I can't afford to have a comfortable environment?" My wife responded, "Exactly. When you were gainfully employed, I put up with your obsession for heat, but now that you are retired we are going to have to cut some corners." Trust me, if my wife were appointed the energy czar, the country would not have an energy problem.

On the second day of my retirement, I was completely blindsided by my wife's behavior. She was vacuuming the upstairs bedrooms when I noticed that the mail truck had arrived at our house. I picked up the mail from the box, sorted it out, and placed my wife's mail on the kitchen table. When she came downstairs, I casually mentioned that I had retrieved the mail, and that hers was on the kitchen table. Based on the look on her face, you would have thought that I had announced that I had sold our children into slavery.

I realized something was wrong, but I did not have a clue what the problem was. I asked her why she seemed so upset. She replied, "I have been getting the mail every day that we have been married. It's part of my daily routine. I like going through all the mail and then distributing it to you and the kids." Being the sensitive husband that I am, I replied, "Are you kidding me? Unless you are having an affair with the mail carrier, or have a secret fantasy to work as a postal clerk, who cares who gets the mail?" Before she could answer, I asked her another question. "What should I do when the mail is delivered and I am home and you are still at work?" She replied, "Just let it sit in the mailbox. I will retrieve it when I return home."

This conversation seemed pretty wacky to me, but I asked the next logical question which I thought was rhetorical in nature. "You don't mind if I get my own mail out of the box, do you? " "Yes, I do," she firmly replied. "Don't worry about the mail. It will be one less thing that you have to worry about." I realized I wasn't going to win this argument. At that moment I gained a much deeper appreciation for George Burns and understood what it must have been like being married to Gracie.

Fortunately, my retirement has been wonderful and the biggest reason is my wife. She enjoys her job (jobs) and loves the freedom we have to be able to travel and vacation together. Most importantly, she doesn't resent the fact that she works and I don't. She actually encourages me to go out and play. I must admit I think she has an ulterior motive. When she is subbing at school, and her friends start talking about, make that complaining about their spouses, my wife listens patiently. When it is her turn, there is no contest. All the woman start feeling better about their husbands while my wife is being considered for sainthood.

If you decide not to work during retirement, having a network of friends who also do not punch a clock is vital to make the process work. Now, some people can retire and fill their time amusing themselves by reading, working around the house, etc. Others are so outgoing and aggressive, they have the ability to quickly forge new relationships and friendships. However, my experience demonstrates that these people account for 5% of the population. Most people do not want to be isolated and cut off from the socialization aspect. Yet at 50 or 60 years old we are not too motivated or interested in developing a new network of friends, especially at the cost of diluting our present relationships.

I have several friends who took early retirement and chose not to pursue another full-time career. A couple of friends have their own businesses, and they work out of their houses. Unfortunately, still others have been laid off from their jobs during the depressed economy, giving them a lot of discretionary time off. This motley crew creates a great opportunity to roll the clock back and do things during the week that haven't been possible since our college days.

Remember a time before computers, instant messaging, and mobile phones? You were a little kid and if you wanted to play with one of your friends, you went over to his house or apartment, knocked on the door and asked your friend's mom if Karl could come out to play. Well, basically that's what I do now. However, instead of talking to Karl's mom, I now speak to Karl's wife. The conversation, 50 years later, is pretty much the same. "Hi, Judy, can Karl go out and play today?" "I don't know, he has a lot of chores to do around the house." Karl picks up the phone, and talks to his wife and me simultaneously. "Hi, Pat. Come on, hun, I will do the chores when I get back. I won't be late." I can hear Judy's voice in the background. "Oh, go ahead. But if you don't finish the errands, you're in hot water." Five minutes later, Karl is out of the house. Some things never change.

CHAPTER 4
Typical Day

People often ask me, "Now that you are retired and don't have a job, how do you keep busy?" Many other new retirees have repeated the response I give: "I'm so busy I can't believe I had time to work full-time for all those years. I start the day by sleeping late in the morning (8:30). Why should I get up early? I am not punching a clock. I have no set schedule, and getting a good night's sleep is beneficial to my health. I shower, dress, and do all of the usual am rituals.

My first activity of the day is my five-minute workout. Yes, I shower prior to my exercise. Let's face it, how sweaty can you get in five minutes? The next thing I do is to get online with my computer. I read my e-mails, which largely consists of jokes from my working friends who obviously have a lot of spare time on their hands, and advertisements that guarantee that I will become a better lover, lose weight, or be able to watch all the premium cable channels for free. By the time I check the news, sports, and the stock market, the morning is slowly starting to disappear.

My next chore is to set up sports and luncheon appointments for the week. Once you stop working, you become the social secretary for your friends. After all, they are working hard for a living, and you're basically a bum with nothing to do. The golf tee-off times are particularly tricky. Dennis can't make Tuesday morning, but he's a definite maybe for Thursday.

Wednesday looks good for Jerry, but he is out for Thursday. Al is wide open for the week, but if his meetings get rescheduled, he is out. Neil wants to play nine holes, but everyone else wants to play 18 holes. Mike wants to know where we are playing on Sunday. Now this is stress!

An hour later, all the pieces of the puzzle are put together and you run out the door to have lunch with a friend. You have a stimulating intellectual discussion pondering the mysteries of life. Will the Yankees make that blockbuster deal? Are the Rangers ever going to make the playoffs? Who has a better chance to make the Super Bowl—Giants or Jets? Satisfied that you have solved mankind's most pressing problems, you head back home just-in-time to tackle one of the many household chores that are written in bold letters on your "to do" list, courtesy of your wife.

The rest of the week is filled up with golf, racquetball, tennis, and basketball. You trade off a great aerobic workout doing the things you enjoy for sore feet, back pain, and tennis elbow. The pain is well worth it.

A special note regarding golf, if you retire and play the game, a note of caution: you will get no respect from your friends who are not retired. If you play well, they are unimpressed. "Of course you play well, you play three, four times a week, and when you're not playing you are beating balls on the practice range." If you play poorly, they will treat you like a rented mule. "Pat, you are a disgrace; you play three or four times a week. Is this is the best you can do? You stink! If I played as often as you, I would be on the Senior tour." On the weekends, your friends who have real jobs and can't play during the week are chomping at the bit to play on Saturday or Sunday. They expect you to set up the golf outing, and they don't seem to be concerned that the same course that I played during the week will now cost me twice as much for the right to socialize with these weekend warriors.

On the plus side, there are advantages to being retired when it comes to golf. Everybody and his brother have your name on their lists when they are organizing a golf outing. While I do love to play the game and my schedule is not restricted because of work demands, it is not practical to accept all of these invitations. The same thing holds true for golf trips, usually four or five day adventures to Myrtle Beach or somewhere in Florida during the cold weather months. Financially, it is impossible to participate in all of these golf trips. Plus, I am afraid that I might discover that my wife has posted my picture on a milk carton. However, the more outings and trips I decline, the more phone calls I get at the last minute encouraging me to join these golf junkets for free. It seems that at the last minute a certain percentage of people always cancel for a variety of reasons. The host of these events needs people to fill these slots and by offering these outings and vacations at reduced or no charge, they can satisfy their quotas and keep the event organized. Someone like me, who needs all of thirty seconds to make a golf commitment, is a prime target for these last minute invitations.

Recently, this same scenario unfolded and provided me with one of my most unusual golf experiences. My friends, Zeke and Judy Pitson, were celebrating their 25th wedding anniversary. Judy at the last minute decided to give her husband a golf trip to Kiawah Island, South Carolina, to both play golf and be a spectator at the World Cup Golf Tournament. The tournament consists of two-man teams from a host of countries and every day the teams play a different format: best ball, alternate shot, etc. Judy was so confident that I would accept her invitation to go on the golf trip with Zeke, that she booked the vacation and then asked me to accompany Zeke. Well, I would have liked to have more time to reschedule my calendar, but Zeke and I have been the closest of friends for 45 years and if I could contribute to Zeke and Judy's happiness in some small way, I would make the sacrifice.

Once we arrived at the resort, we immediately headed for the links. We played Turtle Point, a beautiful golf course. Zeke was struggling all day, which came as no surprise to me, but didn't diminish the frustration that he was suffering. The best thing that can be said for Zeke's golf game is that he is a gifted C.P.A. When he plays golf with a client, the client instantly feels confident that Zeke must spend countless hours in the office meticulously watching over his business (he does), leaving little time to master a game that cannot be mastered. We headed over to the 15th tee, a par 4. The layout of the hole is beautiful. You drive into a relatively narrow fairway. On your left is a fence which separates the golf course from the beach and the Atlantic Ocean. On the right side of the fairway are magnificent homes. The fortunate owners can watch both the trials and tribulations of golfers attempting to defeat this hole, and beyond the golf course, view the Atlantic Ocean.

Zeke crushes his drive, but unfortunately he hooks the ball over the fence and heading towards the ocean. Zeke, ever the optimist, believes the ball may have hit the fence and landed safely. Ten minutes later, Zeke finally gives up his Don Quixote search for the lost golf ball, inspired by the foursome behind us, who are threatening us with bodily harm if we don't pick up the pace of play. We finish the round and now flash forward two days later, same golf course and same hole. Zeke tees off and this time puts the ball in play. His second shot is a good one, but at the last minute, it fades and goes to the right of the green. Our foursome finds itself in what has become a familiar activity, the Easter egg-like hunt for Zeke's golf ball.

We direct our search in the shrubs and trees that guard a beautiful ocean view mansion that overlooks the green. There is a group of people sunbathing on the veranda above us, eating and drinking and having a good time. We can't help hearing their conversation, as they are literally located about 15 feet above our heads.

One fellow, obviously a guest, asks his friend, "Do golfers ever hit the ball over the fence onto the sand and ocean?" His friend replies, "Yes. I walk on the beach often and have seen golf balls buried in the sand. I never pick them up because I don't play this silly game, but a couple of days ago I was walking on the beach and I saw this golf ball with the initials Z.E.K.E written across the ball. I put it into my pocket and figured one of my golfing friends might know what this stands for."

Upon hearing this, Zeke walks out from under the veranda and says, "That's my ball. My name is Zeke," and he proceeds to replay what transpired on the 15th hole two days ago. The people on the deck start laughing, "Yea, right. First of all, nobody is named Zeke, and you're telling us that you lost this ball two days ago and coincidentally you're standing under our deck at the moment my buddy is telling me about the Z.E.K.E. golf ball?" Zeke doesn't answer, and with a wry smile on his face, flips the group a golf ball and says, "Does the ball look something like this?"

The person who found the original ball looks at it dumbfounded, as the balls are an exact match. Our foursome and the people above us are hooting, hollering and high-fiving, (they were also drinking heavily). They invite all of us to join them on the deck. Nobody can even guess what the odds are that this series of events could unfold, (leading to the discovery of the Zeke golf ball.) We decline their invitation as we have three holes to play to finish our round. They wave good-bye and proceed to go inside the house. Zeke shouts at them, "Hey, you forgot to give me back my two golf balls." Embarrassed, they flip the balls down to Zeke, who promptly loses them on the next hole.

Speaking of sports, as Howard Cosell was fond of saying; basketball has been part of my athletic activities since I was a child. Growing up in New York City, basketball is considered the national sport. These days, once a week, I drive an hour to play basketball with a group of guys whose ages range from 33 to 57 years. The older core group has been playing basketball together for the past 25 years. Retirement has allowed me to rejoin the league. After all, you can play three hours of basketball, have a beer, and eat a late dinner, knowing that you don't have to get up at 6:30 a.m. for work.

The basketball games are competitive and entertaining. It's kind of like watching two over-the-hill heavyweight boxers fight. They are slow, out of shape, and their reflexes are shot, but the fighters still believe they are young lions, and since both pugilists have eroded their skills equally, it makes for a competitive, if not a skillful contest. The players who were the best rebounders, scorers, and defensive players 20 years ago, still maintain their positions in the pecking order today. The same lingo and trash talking found in schoolyards and courts across the country is part of our Tuesday night ritual: "Foul." "You're crazy. I got all ball." "That was an illegal pick," "No way, I never moved," "You can't guard me. You'd better switch off before you get embarrassed."

Every once in awhile one of the kids joins us to play. He is usually someone who is in his late twenties or early thirties, who is in good shape and played basketball in either high school or college. For some reason, I always play poorly on those days. I feel physically good, but my legs feel as if they are in quicksand. I spend most of the night apologizing for the numerous fouls and my clutching and grabbing defense, which would make any National Hockey League defenseman proud. Fortunately, I always rebound from these poor performances and regain my speed and quickness. Ironically, these young guns never show up when I am on top of my game.

Retirement not only offers you the opportunity to exercise your body, but also allows you the time to exercise your mind. During the course of the day, you have the opportunity to read books. I enjoyed reading when I was young, but in later years my focus centered on the sports page, takeout menus, and directions for installing various electronic equipment. Sadly, I have not taken advantage of my leisure time to devour the extensive library of books that continues to gather dust in my living room. I have, however, become a magazine scholar. Every month I pour through numerous golf magazines and several financial publications. What is my reward for this newfound love of reading? My golf swing is on life support. After reading conflicting advice and implementing a variety of drills and techniques, I can barely lift the club away from the ball. As I prepare to hit the ball little voices chirp inside my head, "Slow and low. Keep your left arm straight, make a full turn, start the downswing with your legs, or do you drop your hands first? Stay on plane. What is the plane?" My golf swing has been grounded.

The financial magazines confirmed what I had already assumed. "Experts" in the field, armed with extensive financial tools have the ability to pick and recommend dog stocks, just as I do. The magazines, like all publications, were filled with ads.

I was drawn to the huge advertisements supplied by various mutual fund companies. Even in the bleakest of economic times these firms flaunt their incredible rate of return that their investors have received. This only gets me angry. I immediately pull out my calculator and determine how much more money I would have accumulated if I had utilized the firm in the advertisement. This exercise is very similar to the mental gymnastics that you perform when you are told that someone you knew had passed away. You immediately, in your head, calculate the number of years that the deceased is older or younger than you and, just like reading the financial advertisement, you often start to feel ill. I considered purchasing significant shares from one prominent mutual fund that constantly advertised in every magazine that I read. I wasn't expecting to make money on the purchase. Rather, my objective was to expose the fund when it cashed my check and of course took the inevitable nose dive in performance. After further review, becoming penniless to prove a point was not a very smart financial strategy, and it was quickly abandoned.

Sometimes, seemingly the most insignificant activities afforded by retirement give you great pleasure. When they are employed, most people either don't have time to eat lunch, or because of their job description entertain clients at restaurants on a consistent basis. Now that I am retired, I look forward to going to a drive-through restaurant, parking my car, reclining my seat and turning on the radio. In between munching on a double cheeseburger and fries, I furiously spin the AM dial between sports programming and various talk radio formats. If you are on top of your game at least one of the stations is broadcasting while the others are on commercial. I enjoy this quiet time. I no longer commute to work so this hour gives me my fix of sports and politics. A note of caution: after several weeks of dining on fast food cuisine, I was becoming a candidate for the lead in the movie *Supersize Me.* I have since changed my eating habits, but I must tell you that rice, shredded carrots, and granola are much harder to dislodge from your car seat than fries.

If you spend time at home during the day, beware of that black box in your family room. This device is known by many different names across the globe—El Diablo, Satan, and of course in America, the television. The screen looks innocent enough. It doesn't force you to turn it on. It allows you freedom of choice. What you don't realize is that when you sit down on the couch the box transmits subliminal messages to your brain. "Hey check me out. It doesn't cost anything. I have something on that you are going to love." You are being seduced by an electronic component! I try not to watch television during the course of the day. If I turn the tube on, I am done. These days if you are an addictive channel surfer, as I am, by the time you have made your full cycle, watching snippets of a variety of shows, you can waste close to an hour. Once you finished scrolling, new television shows appear. Now, you figure the odds have to be strongly in your favor that something entertaining is being broadcast somewhere inside that box, and you proceed to start the cycle again. When you finally turn the set off, you have wasted an incredible amount of time and your razor sharp mind has turned into a limp celery stalk. My rule of thumb is to never watch television before 7:30 at night. Once you hunker down for your evening entertainment, you can watch all of your sports entertainment, and hopefully, find some quality programming among the 200 or so channels that are at your disposal.

That being said, can you believe the junk that is being broadcast today? There must be 25 so-called reality shows being aired. I thought that one of the virtues of television, like the movies, was to entertain you and give you the opportunity to escape reality for a short period of time. If I were motivated to watch people eat insects, I could put a chair in front of my house during the summer months and watch the neighborhood kids dine on organisms that would be too graphic to show on television. If I had an appetite to observe families cursing and fighting with one another, I would get in my car and visit one of my relatives.

But not all television is bad. When I first retired and had time on my hands I looked forward to watching *Jeopardy* on a daily basis. What a mistake that turned out to be! I remember reading that as you age, your brain cells continue to die. I don't know how they scientifically validated that claim, but if you observe Baby Boomers playing *Jeopardy* and compare their performance with years gone by, you will have all the proof you need. I'm still pretty good at *Jeopardy*, as long as I'm given at least 5 minutes to respond to the answers. 75% of the time I am sure that I know the correct question; however, for some inexplicable reason the super highway that runs from my head to my vocal cords is always congested and all thoughts must proceed with caution. At no time is this handicap more evident than the nights that my son Jay challenges me to a *Jeopardy* match. Thankfully, he doesn't possess the correct information often, but when he does, he responds with the question before Alex finishes reading the answer. My responses to his warp speed skills are very mature, "That's not fair, and you cheated. I knew the answer, I just didn't say it." My advice to retired Boomers, to avoid embarrassment and humiliation, is to play with someone your own age.

There are several television networks that are wildly popular with retired Boomers. The Weather Channel and the Home Shopping Network are two of the most prominent. This is our generation's MTV, and to me, this is very scary! In the past, I would complain to friends that my wife was fixated on the Weather Channel. To my surprise, they not only admitted they watched the program regularly, but gave me their opinion and feedback on the various meteorologists who forecast the weather. These weather reporters have actually achieved some sort of cult status with the over-50 crowd. But my pet peeve is, how quickly does the weather forecast change? If I were floating on a raft in the middle of the Pacific Ocean, you can be assured that my ear would be tuned to the updated weather forecast. Maybe it's me, but once I hear the weather prediction, I am good to go for the rest of the day. I'm taking my chances that the blizzard of the century or the second coming of the flood is not going to appear on the Doppler radar screen for the next twelve hours. I must admit that I find it amusing when a weather channel groupie shows up at the golf course with shorts and sunglasses and is soon soaked when the unforeseen rain shower occurs. If you want a weather forecast, open your window and stick your head outside. Your chances to predict the weather correctly are about the same as the high tech weatherman.

The Home Shopping Network, like the Weather Channel, has universal appeal for both men and women. The female Boomers can purchase fashion, jewelry, and a host of other big ticket items and yet still somehow manage to have the time to order that special pocket knife or mini flashlight for the man in their lives. Some might argue that the female shoppers may buy these token gifts for their partners to rationalize the impressive credit card bill that will be arriving at the house in the coming weeks. But, I'm sure the women appreciate that love doesn't have to come in large packages; it's the thought that counts.

To be fair, men make their share of purchases from the HSN as well. However, we have an excuse. We are a captive audience. No matter where we go in the house we hear the faint sales pitch of the shows' spokesman hawking dresses, lingerie, and gem stones. Finally, the segment changes and they are selling the electronics or sporting equipment that we are interested in. Normally, we wouldn't watch this channel in a million years. But when you realize that they are selling a 2.8 gigahertz computer with 512 megabyte of RAM, utilizing 160 gigabytes hard drive with a DVD/CD combo and a 17" flat screen for less than $1,000, you have to sit up and take notice.

There is another network that is solely for the use and entertainment of the fairer sex, America's Choice Network, also affectionately known as the *bling bling* network. This concern sells jewelry and gemstones 24 hours a day. Men, this network is dangerous to your financial health and has been the source of many failed marriages. Every woman craves jewelry. It doesn't matter if they are fat or thin, young or old, jewelry always works.

I always know when my wife is watching ACN because I hear moans and groans that are usually associated with late night cable movies. The gemstone world has its own vocabulary. ACN speaks to my wife in a foreign tongue, using terms that I have never heard before: rubalight, tanzanite, tourmaline, helenite. Are these new gem stones that have miraculously been unearthed, or new additions to the Periodic table?

If you continually expose yourself to radiation, something bad is going to happen to you. If you watch this network constantly, something bad is going to happen to your bank account. You are going to purchase jewelry—probably more than you need and maybe more than you can afford. There is however a very interesting dynamic that seems to be consistent with the women to whom I spoke about this subject—a silver lining on the cloud of addictive shopping if you will. Many shoppers return as much jewelry as they purchase. Sometimes the size or color is not to their liking or they realized that their purchase was impulsively made, but I suspect there is a third explanation. Women love to receive gifts, and jewelry is their favorite gift. Realistically, how many wives are surprised with gifts of any kind from husbands? If your wife's answer is yes, she is in an exclusive sorority; She had better keep close tabs on her husband because he's a keeper. I believe that women enjoy the excitement and the anticipation of opening a gift as much as they covet the item contained in the box. Hence, returning the jewelry is not as dramatic as you would expect. What does all of this mean? I haven't a clue. It makes me regret that I missed most of my psychology courses as a college student.

Rivaling the black box for your leisure time enjoyment is the Internet. Yes, the same tool that was a key element of your job performance when you were gainfully employed. Remember, emailing and instant messaging your friends, downloading questionable material, and reading every joke that had ever been written? This was no easy feat considering that the possibility always existed that your boss could magically appear and crash your party. You are retired now. There is no need to continue your covert activities. Take full advantage of all that the Internet has to offer. The downside is that nobody pays you for performing these job-related skills.

The Internet offers retired Baby Boomers a myriad of choices for spending their newly discovered free time. Just learning or strengthening your computer skills to engage in technology-oriented activities is an exciting challenge. Could our parents ever have conceived of the concept of participating in an online Texas Hold' Em Poker game, or cleaning out their house and selling their junk for money on eBay? Even visionaries could not predict that one day, through no fault of your own, Microsoft would constantly send you error messages claiming you were engaged in unlawful activities, and boot you off the internet.

The computer-user community is really divided into two groups. The first group is a small but determined force who seems to possess unlimited computer skills, and if given enough time, can solve any technical problem thrown its way. Let's call this group Gurus. The second group is much larger, has no interest in building computer skills, and is generally lazy and just wants the problem fixed. Let's call this group Bewildered. If you are Bewildered, then you better have access to your own Guru. Once you have stamped your mark on your Guru, never let him out of your sight. If he is going out of town, he should notify you in advance and email you contact information. This is the person who is going to prevent you from tossing your computer out of the window. He is a deity and must be treated as such. Here is a tip for my fellow Bewildered brethren: Gurus are constantly harassed and solicited by many people. For expediency, they will attempt to solve your problem over the phone. Don't get sucked into this ploy. You will waste hours of time and your frustration level will reach the boiling point. If you could execute complicated commands over the phone you would be moving out of the Bewildered group, and let's face it, you're not going anywhere! Once the Guru is in your home, sitting at your computer, your heavy lifting is over. Go watch the ball game on television. It doesn't make sense that both of you should get frustrated. Be polite, from time to time get off the couch and ask him if there is anything you could help with. If he is a true Guru, he will be focused on his task and oblivious that you are present. At some point, he will solve the unsolvable problem. He will have gained a tremendous sense of self-satisfaction and you will be able to return to cyberspace to explore the mysteries of the Internet.

But, beware! The Internet is the younger sister of the black box. She can become habit forming. It's not uncommon for a retiree to spend hours surfing the web on a daily basis. Please surf responsibly! To sum it up, retired Baby Boomers have opportunities that present themselves on a daily basis. If you have a zest for life, and embrace new experiences, boredom will not be your companion.

CHAPTER 5
Physical Fitness/Nutrition

Retirement gives you the time to do things that were difficult to fit into your schedule when you were working. You needed to get more exercise when you were working, but you just did not have the time. Now you have the time and no longer have an excuse. Let's get fit! What is the right exercise regime for you? Should you buy some of the in-home gym equipment that is being hawked on the cable television channels? Join a health club? Buy fitness tapes and work out at home? Who cares? Any of the physical fitness options will work. The challenge is for you to pick a plan that will motivate you to adhere to it religiously. You already know this, so make some sort of physical conditioning part of your daily routine. You will lose weight, gain strength, and have more energy.

The data on physical fitness for the Baby Boomer generation is encouraging, disappointing, and confusing all at the same time. The results from the annual Baby Boomer Report conducted by Del Webb in April of 2003 reported that of the 1,361 Baby Boomers who completed their survey, 88% felt that they would be happier in retirement if they remained physically active; 60% reported exercising at least once a week; and 93% expected to exercise the same amount or more in retirement.

That's the good news. The reality is that obesity has

increased dramatically during the past 15 years and as of 2001 the chubbiest segment of the population are people 50-59. According to the Centers for Disease Control, 25% of Boomers in this category are considered overweight. However, you don't need government statistics to validate this claim. Take a stroll in your local shopping mall or any place where large numbers of people gather, and you will observe a significant number of overweight parents. Sadly, these parents are surrounded by their overweight children, which does not bode well for the future. The most damning statistical evidence is that two out of three Americans are overweight, and five out of six are out of shape.

Where did my crack research staff uncover this information? Actually, I don't have a research staff, but my source is unimpeachable. Chuck Norris mouthed these words during a late night infomercial. If you dispute his claim, he will be happy to karate kick some sense into you! Yankelovich Partners have been conducting polls for the past 30 years. Their 2003 report on consumer behavior, the *Yankelovich Monitor,* highlighted health-related activities that Boomers "care about" vs. those they are "currently doing." As an example, 68% of those surveyed care about being the proper weight, but only 47% of the people are doing anything to achieve a healthy weight. 52% care about exercising, but only 37% exercise. 45% care about reducing fat in their diet, but only 22% actually reduce the fat in their diet. In other words, Baby Boomers have identified what is important and what corrective action they should implement to promote a healthy lifestyle, but many of us are too lazy or unwilling to change our behavior. To some, this information is disturbing, but to me it's great news. I am not alone!

Not being the most motivated person in the world, I

developed my own work-out regime. I call it the 5-MINUTE WORK OUT. I do it 5 times a week. (I thought 7 times a week would be overkill.) The beauty of my fitness routine is that you can always find 5 minutes a day to exercise, even if you are still working full time. However, I must confess that if I do not get my workout completed in the morning, my chances of finishing my workout decrease dramatically. If you were ambitious, my 5-minute work out could actually be completed in three minutes, but I allow myself two minutes to daydream and rest between exercises. I utilize the ab roller, a simple but effective device to work the mid section. I do 40 stomach crunches, 12 side crunches, (both sides) and 12 crunches raising the knees to the chest. Next, I will do 12 curls with barbells (both arms) or a similar strength building exercise. If I had any drive, I would complete my session with 45 minutes on the treadmill. This would give me the perfect complement of anaerobic and aerobic exercise. The treadmill and the universal gym located in the basement have become rusted due to lack of use, but they serve as a great place to hang and dry the laundry. I could petition my wife to remove the garments from the equipment and really accelerate my workout, but then what kind of a spouse would I be? I would rather forfeit 45 minutes of sweat and pain than see my wife unhappy. I tell people about the 5-minute workout, and they think I am kidding. I am not. It works!

I knew I was on to something with my workout program, when several years ago I was browsing through a bookstore in Orlando, Florida, and my eye caught a glimpse of a book called THE 8 MINUTE WORK OUT. I thought, "this guy is using my idea and adding 3 minutes to the workout; or maybe my ingenious workout is only five-eighths as good as his, but saves you 3 minutes a day." I picked up the book. It was thick and filled with information. I thought maybe there was some merit to what I was doing as well as some lasting benefits.

In addition, I play all kinds of sports. I do not necessarily play them well, but I enjoy any game where you have to chase a ball. Basketball, tennis, racquetball, and golf fill this void for me and give me the aerobic exercise that is needed. I acquired this skill as a child. My father would throw various objects to me (at me) and I was instructed to run as fast as I could and fetch them. To this day, I cannot walk by a fire hydrant with out feeling uncomfortable. Speaking of my dad, he is a physical fitness nut. (I take after my mother.) My father just turned 81 and he continues to exercise relentlessly. He devised his own workout program and exercises three times a week. The program combines calisthenics and riding a stationary bike. To keep from getting bored, he rotates his exercises in an organized fashion. His workout regimen combined with walking on the golf course has made him extremely fit. Obviously I am too young to perform this exacting workout schedule, but I look forward to the day when I will be old enough to meet this rigorous challenge.

Nutrition and fitness go hand in hand. You need to exercise and eat sensibly. The best advice on the subject comes from the famous Italian philosopher, Ann Paciello, my mother. When queried on how to lose weight, she replied, "Easy, buy smaller plates and put smaller portions on the plate." Jack LaLanne, a pioneer for better health and fitness since what seems like the beginning of time, offers these words. "You've got to eat right, exercise, and have goals and challenges. Exercise is king, nutrition is queen, put them together and you have a kingdom!" These days there is a plethora of new diet plans. Every week there is a revolutionary diet formula that captures the fancy of the public (Atkins, South Beach, etc,). It is only a matter of time before you see on the bestseller shelves of your local bookstore the amazing EAT ANYTHING DIET. You consume anything that you can stuff your face with. Eventually this will induce a coma. You will be fed intravenously, and worked out five times a week by your own personal cyborg trainer. You wake up 2-3 years later, lean and fit. Nutrition, like fitness, is simply mind over matter. Any diet plan that reduces your intake of fats, carbohydrates and calories (the bad things), will work. It's up to you to pick a plan that is reasonable and gives you the best opportunity to continue with the diet. This of course is easier said than done. Is there anyone on the planet who doesn't know that cigarette smoking is harmful to your health? Yet, we see people of all ages still lighting up. We have all witnessed someone who constantly gorges himself as if tomorrow is his date with the electric chair. It is amazing how many of these same people faced with life or death consequences, find the motivation to change their eating and life style habits.

The one diet from my own experience that seems to work very effectively is the wedding diet. The wedding diet is almost 100% effective for women and approximately 50% successful for men. The key to the plan is to be married, and have children. Your children will most likely get married. As Baby Boomers, our children are approaching this most wonderful of times. There is not a mother of the bride or groom on this planet who doesn't want to look good for her child's wedding. Who wants to stare at the wedding album and gaze at the photos on the dresser and think, "I really look fat!" If you don't like your appearance, you will be reminded of that fact on a daily basis. Let's face it ladies, consciously or subconsciously, you want to look better than the mother of your son or daughter's spouse. You want to hear comments like,"She looks so young to have a married daughter, or she must have gotten married at a really young age." The motivation to look good is incredible. Women, who formerly never owned a pair of sneakers, are now hitting the gym, jogging around the neighborhood, and following a sensible diet. The excuses parroted for the past twenty years ("I have no time to exercise. It is harder for a woman to lose weight than for a man. Eating chocolate cheesecake at 10 o'clock at night makes me happy. Don't you want me to be happy?") disappear in a heart beat with new-found determination.

Men on the other hand, are not quite as motivated. Sure, we want to look good for the wedding, but we have a secret weapon—the tuxedo! Prior to the wedding, we start to change our eating and exercising habits for the better, but that usually lasts until we get fitted for the tuxedo. Once we drape the jacket and fasten the accessories on, and realize that the clothing hides our gut pretty well, we echo our own rationalizations: "I don't look so bad. Nobody's looking at me anyway. Besides, my job is to write the check and make sure that the guests have a good time."

If you follow the wedding plan, you will achieve your objectives; however, it is vital to continue with some sort of maintenance program after the marriage. The reasons are obvious, but the wedding diet offers an ironic caveat. As the years pass and you look at the wedding pictures, if you have not continued with proper diet and exercise, your thoughts will be, "I looked good at the wedding. How did I let myself go so quickly?"

On the same subject of nutrition, I am very impressed with how many seniors organize their meal plans. If you do a lot of traveling, you will invariably find yourself dining at restaurants at off hours. (4:30—6:00 PM). You scan the patrons. You can count the number of people who are younger than 60 on one hand and you do not even need all your fingers.

I always assumed that seniors ate early to take advantage of the early bird special. Believe me, that is true and God bless them. They also do not have to wait 45 minutes for a table. Most importantly, many have modified their eating schedules to promote a healthier life style. Conventional medical advice today suggests that we should eat four or five small meals during the course of the day. Many seniors that I have observed eat a substantial breakfast in the morning, skip lunch and have an early dinner. In both cases, the key is to avoid snacking on junk food. By eating two meals a day and giving the digestive process a longer time to work before bedtime, they reap health benefits that are sadly lacking for most of us. Now that I am older and a retiree myself, I see the wisdom of the elderly.

The last piece of the wellness puzzle is our present day health care system. We all know that the health-care system needs to be revamped. No question that lower income retirees have to make choices between medication and food. However, my concern is how middle and upper income retirees utilize the present medical system. Our parents, who justly deserve the moniker The Greatest Generation, are contributing to part of the problem. The retirees of today enjoy a unique relationship with medical practitioners .A visit to the doctor's office has become as commonplace as early bird specials, cutting out coupons, and spending winters in sunny Florida. Many seniors visit different doctors multiple times during the week. Of course, some of the care is necessary, but my observations demonstrate that many doctor visits are redundant, and excessive. If people who could afford to pay for medical benefits were not subsidized, the extraneous medical visits would decline and medical costs would decrease. That is only half of the problem—the retirees of today are armed and dangerous with their multiple pillboxes, often misplacing and mishandling their medications. The doctors contribute to this mess by prescribing medication for the smallest of ills. The worst part though, is that retirees are ingesting so much medication that very often the side effects of the drug are worse than the affliction it was supposed to cure. As the newly retired, let's bring some sanity to this out-of-control problem. Take medication judiciously and utilize the preventive measures of diet, exercise, and nutrition to create a sound mind and body.

CHAPTER 6
Timesharing

As Baby Boomers approaching retirement, the opportunity exits to increase travel and vacation plans. The decision to purchase timeshare weeks is a topic of much debate. I am a believer in purchasing timeshare weeks. I purchased my first week in 1979 in the Pocono Mountains in Pennsylvania, and now have 7 weeks. The timeshare industry in the old days had a very poor reputation (some would say that is true today). The black eye the industry suffered was not that the purchase of timesharing was a poor or fraudulent investment; rather, the marketing practice to lure you into visiting their property was deceptive and misleading—the classic bait and switch gambit that is common in advertising.

The process went something like this. You would receive in the mail an invitation to visit a resort. However this invitation often failed to inform the individual that the purpose of the solicitation was to induce you to purchase timeshare weeks. To entice you to come they guaranteed that you would win one of several possible gifts. The gifts were presented in the following manner:

You are guaranteed to receive one of the following:
(a) $1,000 in cash
(b)   27" color television (Big screens didn't exist)
(c)   Brand new car

(d)   Vacation in the Caribbean

(e)   Pendant

Getting something for nothing appeals to most people, and who knows, maybe, just maybe, you might win the top prize. After listening to the sales presentation and touring the resort, which was a waste of time since you didn't have any money to purchase anything, finally your prize was selected. Of course, nobody ever won the cash, the car, or the television. You either won three days at a nondescript hotel in the Caribbean where the airfare was not included, or a pendant with a retail value of about $10.00. The gifts were useless. You wasted an entire Saturday or Sunday and felt that you were misled and deceived. There were a lot of unhappy campers who trashed the whole timeshare industry. Fortunately, the industry and the government cleaned up these shady marketing tactics. Today, you must deal with a new set of challenges in the marketing of the timeshare industry, but I will address this new battle later on in the chapter.

Buying timeshare weeks makes good sense for Baby Boomers and their children. Timeshare weeks can cost from $3,000 to $40,000 per week. You own the use of one week of vacation ownership at the particular resort from which you have purchased. You can purchase anything from a studio unit to a 4-bedroom unit. You can purchase multiple weeks. The week is generally deeded property, so you can pass on the ownership to your heirs.

I am going to assume that you are familiar with the basics of timesharing. If I go into minute detail, I will bore myself to sleep. Besides, if you have not received some timeshare solicitation over your lifetime, you either live in a cave, or have entered this country illegally.

Timeshare ownership makes sense for the following reasons:

(a) Economics—The price of vacations is going through the roof. You are retiring; you want to take more vacations and travel more. When you compare the price of vacations at the same resort, timeshare versus hotel guest, you will vacation more inexpensively by being an owner rather than a guest and will have significantly more space in your living quarters.

(b) Once you purchase a week or weeks, your children and grandchildren will want to come on vacation with you. If you bought a unit that is big enough, (2, 3, 4 bedrooms) they can visit without any additional cost to you.

(c) If you so desire, you can give your week to your children. This makes a great wedding gift, and now your children can take you on vacation and you will no longer pay maintenance fees. I will discuss this later.

(d) Travel options—All timeshare resorts are members of a vacation exchange program (RCI and Interval International being the two largest). Having the ability to vacation at different resorts at different times of the year increases your vacation experience.

(e) Boomer power—Being retired, you have a unique advantage as to how you can utilize the timeshare network that others do not. You have the availability to vacation whenever you like and without a lot of notice. This flexibility pays dividends in vacation ownership. You not only can exchange your week to visit other quality resorts, but you can vacation in resorts where the demand makes it almost impossible to exchange. The reason is that the retired Boomer has the flexibility to vacation at non-peak or off-season times.

(f) Bonus weeks—Every timeshare resort has the ability to offer you what they call bonus or vacation weeks. These bonus weeks give you the opportunity to enjoy a week's vacation for only the cost of an exchange fee, which is paid to and administered by an RCI or an Interval. These weeks do not require you to exchange the weeks that you own.

(g) Rental weeks—As members of RCI or Interval you will be allowed to rent a week of vacation time at discounted rates from selected resorts. Like bonus weeks, you will not have to exchange the weeks that you own.

(h) Discounted cruises—By exchanging your timeshare week, (give up the use of the week, and pay an exchange fee) you can enjoy vacation cruises at discounted rates.

(i) Points—Recently, a number of resorts have offered points ownership for the week that you have purchased. With points ownership, your week is worth a certain amount of points. You can exchange these points within a network of resorts. The resorts, hotels, etc, all are designated a specific amount of points. If your resort is worth 10,000 points and you want to exchange the week for a resort that is worth 5000 points, you can make the exchange and still have 5000 points in the bank to use for an additional vacation. Conversely; if your resort is worth 10,000 points and you want to exchange your week for a one week stay at the finest hotel in Europe, worth

40,000 points, you save your points to accumulate the number of points that will be needed to take your dream vacation. With this system, you are not required to vacation for a week. You can stay at a resort for as little as one-day, a long weekend, etc. Vacation points are deducted from the points that you own. Marriot, Hilton, and some of the other large hotel chains have emerged as leaders in the timeshare industry. By offering purchasers the opportunity to exchange their week for company owned hotel and timesharing properties via points, they have assured buyers a level of flexibility and quality.

However, timesharing is certainly not for everyone. There are pitfalls and concerns that must be weighed before purchasing your weeks:

(a)   Maintenance fees—You will be paying a yearly maintenance fee and real estate tax. Remember you own the week (deeded property). Generally, the maintenance fee runs from $350 to $700 per week and the real estate tax costs less than $100. The maintenance fee goes to the improvement and repair of the resort facility.

(b)   Exchange fees—To be able to swap your week for another resort through your exchange broker, you will pay an exchange fee. Today that fee is around $139. RCI and Interval charge you a yearly fee to become a member of their respective exchange services (about $100 a year). They offer multi-year discounts if you contract with them for longer periods of time.

(c)   Quality—Make sure that the resort where you purchase is financially strong. Does the company own other resorts? How long has the firm been selling timeshare weeks? It doesn't happen often, but resorts can go belly up or not deliver future amenities that they promised when you purchased your week.

(d) Right place, right time—Purchase a week that you feel comfortable you will utilize often, as opposed to one that you expect to be exchanging often. Remember the exchange fee. Do not be swayed to purchase a more inexpensive week in the off-season if you want to vacation in prime season. For example, you purchase a week on Hilton Head Island in December, but really want to go there in July. The week in July is more expensive than the week in December. You think you beat the system—Wrong! Your chances are slim and none, and slim left town! There is no guarantee that you will be able to exchange your week. If your trading power is weak, you will not be able to exchange for a quality resort in primetime.

(e) Natural Disaster—Resorts along the coastal lines are susceptible to hurricanes, etc. It doesn't happen often, but your vacation can be disrupted if Mother Nature is in a bad mood.

(f) Timeshare weeks are deeded property, but do not purchase a week and expect it to appreciate in value. With few exceptions, you will be lucky to recoup your investment if you decide to sell your week. The legal cost and the broker commissions associated with the sale will eliminate any profit margin. On the other hand, there is a growing market to purchase timeshare resale weeks. As the buyer, you can negotiate a lower price for the week. The downside is that the week will not be offered with the extra bonus weeks or free points and you do not have the same feeling of confidence that you would have by dealing directly with the resort.

How to Beat the System

I recommend buying one week of timesharing at a resort where you feel you will vacation often. You will or have received many timeshare solicitations in the mail. Something like, "Preview our magnificent resort for 3 days, 2 nights and the cost is only $99 per couple. You will be required to participate in a 90-minute sales presentation. There is no obligation to purchase anything." Most people throw these solicitations away, but a person who is retired and has the flexibility of time can take advantage of this travel opportunity.

Today, to market timeshare, they offer these inexpensive mini-week vacations, free dinner at the resort, reduced golf fees, etc., and a bonus vacation just for previewing their resort. If you go on these trips, you will see different resorts in different parts of the country. You can piggyback these visits with other vacation plans and may decide to purchase timeshare. The resorts market themselves this way because it is cost-effective for them. They know that once you visit their resort, there is a reasonable chance that you will purchase. Let me get back to the bonus vacation, which is a feature that I have utilized many times over the years. Most resorts will give you a bonus vacation just for coming to the sales presentation and many times include bonus weeks as an incentive to purchase with them.

For example, I bought a week in Arizona. I received a bonus week for coming to the presentation and three bonus weeks, one each year, for purchasing at the resort. I own in a resort in Williamsburg, Virginia, and receive multiple bonus weeks for every year that I do not utilize the resort (up to a maximum of 10 years). Note: You cannot return to your home resort to receive these bonus weeks, so you exchange your week, thereby creating additional vacation time. These bonus weeks, as I mentioned earlier in the chapter, are unused inventory weeks that an RCI or Interval controls. The naïve purchaser of timeshare gets all excited about these free weeks of vacation. The truth is that unless you have the flexibility of time, you probably won't want to spend one week of your two-week vacation going to the Northeast in early spring or late fall. How can you go on a family vacation while the kids are in school? I have vacationed in magnificent resorts in the middle of December in Hawaii (Maui, Big Island,) Puerto Vallarta, Cape Cod, and Newport Beach, Rhode Island. These properties were wonderful to visit off-season, all for the cost of an exchange fee. The resorts are less crowded and in the case of Hawaii and Mexico, the weather was perfect. These bonus weeks are purchased through RCI or Interval. You must be a member of the exchange service to purchase these weeks. Hence, it is in your best interest to own one week of timeshare to take advantage of the bonus weeks, cruise discounts, etc., etc.

The Sales Pitch

To get the inexpensive vacation and all the perks, you are required to sit through a 90-minute sales presentation. If you have zero interest in purchasing a vacation week, but have one of the following personality traits—guilt, easily persuaded, pride, lack of mental toughness,—then STOP! Stick a fork in yourself! You are done! Skip the remainder of this chapter and continue on with the book. These sales people are the Muhammad Ali's of the real estate world and you are taking your first boxing lesson at the Y. This is no contest!

Most people go the sales presentation thinking, "This is a very nice place, but I am not prepared to purchase today. I don't really want to spend the money. We haven't really looked at other places. Maybe we should buy a vacation home instead of purchasing timeshare weeks." The facts are that if you are visiting a quality resort, there is a good chance that you will purchase. You are in an intoxicating environment. Your friends are shoveling snow back home while you are playing golf on a beautiful course and drinking pina colladas on a veranda overlooking the ocean. What's not to like?

The salesperson is your new best friend. You feel you have known him or her your whole life. You explain that you are not really interested in purchasing, but the resort really is great. He just smiles. You have no idea, but mentally he has already put you in the purchase category for the day. He goes through his pictorial display, backs up his claims with a mountain of statistics and answers all your questions, allays your fears, and seemingly has a solution for all of your concerns.

For example, you say,"I am not sure we can afford the price." His response is, "We can stretch your mortgage over a longer period of time, reducing your monthly payment considerably. We can get you a week that is less expensive, possibly May or June as opposed to July or August. Instead of vacationing every year, you can purchase a unit from us, to utilize every other year, thereby cutting your cost of ownership in half."

The salesperson is wearing you down. Your legs are starting to buckle. You fire a desperation salvo. "We are interested, but we really would like to go home and think about it." The salesperson knows if he doesn't close the deal today, your chances of purchasing are remote. He counters, "To give you this reduced price and additional perks (bonus weeks), you must purchase today. We are required by state law to offer everyone the same package. If you should call in the future, we can sell you the week, but not at this price and without the perks. Remember, if you sign today, by law you have 3 business days to cancel your contract should you change your mind. The salesperson leaves, allowing the couple to talk. Ten minutes later, he returns and you throw in the towel, asking, "Where do I sign?"

Over the years, I have been to over fifty sales presentations to purchase timesharing. The memorable sales presentations included both timeshares that I purchased and ones I did not purchase. One year I purchased a week in Scottsdale, Arizona. The presentation sounded good, but the New Jersey Devils were playing the Dallas Stars in game 5 for the Stanley Cup. Being a big Devils fan, there was no way I was going to miss the game. I told the salesperson I was interested and apologized, but there was no way I was missing the game. He understood, but to close the deal at the discounted price I had to sign today. He said he had no problem finishing the presentation and going through the paperwork while the game was on. During the commercials and between periods, he would gather the necessary information at warp speed. The Devils lost a classic 1-0 game that took 2 overtimes. I jumped up and down on the couch, yelled at the big screen television while the salesperson waited patiently for a break in the action. The game ended, I was physically spent and he was congratulating me for purchasing the week. I didn't hear a word he said, signed documents that I didn't read, and didn't comprehend what I had agreed to until I pulled out the paperwork on the flight home. Fortunately, the purchase ended up making perfect sense for me, and the Devils won the next game to clinch the championship.

Another time I went on a discounted mini-vacation to Williamsburg, Virginia. I told my wife that even if the salesperson sticks pins in us, we must remain strong. We are not going to purchase! Fortunately, the salesperson was a young lady who had just recently been hired. It was quickly evident that I knew far more about the whole process than she did. She started to pick my brain to become more knowledgeable about timesharing. When I told her that I had six weeks of timesharing and couldn't use another week if they gave it to me for free, she quickly agreed. We took a tour of the resort only to satisfy her boss. She made absolutely no effort to sell me anything. I walked around the resort by myself while she chatted with other staff.

We returned to the sales office and she said her supervisor would sit with us as a matter of procedure and then we could pick up our perks and continue with our vacation. The supervisor (a.k.a., the closer) arrived and asked if we would be interested in purchasing a 4-bedroom unit every other year at a terrific price with bonus weeks. The maintenance fee was the same as a two-bedroom unit. What a deal! 20 minutes later I was filling out the paperwork, vowing that this was my final purchase ever. My wife just laughed and reiterated that I was a hopeless case.

The worse sales experience I have ever encountered was at a resort in South Florida. We checked into the resort at 11:30 pm. We had been on the road for about 10 hours and all we wanted to do was sleep. At check in, the service person asked which day would be better to view the resort...Monday or Tuesday? (On an exchange, you are not required to go on a sales presentation). I told my wife and the service person that I had no interest in the sales presentation, but the woman countered that it would take only 30 minutes to see the new units and then fill out a questionnaire. For this small service, you would receive perks including $100 in cash. For a change, I didn't bite, but my wife was insistent. I relented and what followed could only be described as an epic battle of wills, which tested my patience and resolve.

We met the salesperson and explained that we had no interest in purchasing, but would be happy to preview the new units and give our feedback. The salesperson was cheerful and empathetic. (They all are or they wouldn't be in sales). He explained that he was required to go through standard operating procedure and he would have us on our merry way as soon as possible. His presentation took one hour and we had not seen the new villas yet. We reminded him that we were told the whole process would be a half hour. We returned from the villas an hour and a half hour later, irritated, but still friendly and polite.

The salesperson, seeing that we were firm in our convictions, invited the supervisor to sit down with us. I explained our position, again told her that the salesperson did an excellent job and was disappointed that the presentation was far longer and more detailed than was stipulated. She apologized profusely. She blamed the miscommunication on the service people at the front desk and said she would correct that flaw. During our conversation, another couple a little older voiced their complaints to their salesperson. The couple was seated about 20 feet from me echoing exactly the same experience that I was going through. The difference was that this man was angry and he made sure everyone felt his venom. It was ugly, but to my surprise our supervisor continued with her performance. She was good. She used every advanced tactic and strategy contained in the mystical timesharing sales manual. She praised me, "You are obviously a very successful businessman and I am sure that when you saw a good business opportunity, you didn't vacillate. You made the right decision quickly. If you didn't take advantage of opportunities, you wouldn't be retired today, living the comfortable lifestyle you deserve. Isn't that true?" She tried to embarrass me. "Is money the problem?" Can you afford to make a payment of $100 per month? You like the resort. You believe in timesharing. That is correct, isn't it? Is there a financial problem that would prohibit you from purchasing today?"

When I wouldn't budge, she would try to engage my wife into the conversation. "What do you think, Mrs. Paciello? How do you like the resort? What are your interests and activities?" She continued to probe, looking for any sign of weakness or an opening to exploit. The conversation was becoming surreal. It was like a giant chess game with one player attacking, probing, trying to penetrate the defense, and the other player in retreat hoping not to get check-mated and end the game in a draw. I had been on this sales odyssey for 3 ½ hours. I was tired, worn out, hungry, and had wasted one of my vacation days saying no 100 times to people who wouldn't take no for an answer.

Finally, it was over. They coldly sent me to a financial manager to pick up a cash incentive and additional perks. I had been sitting so long that my legs were cramping and I felt sure that if I were held hostage any longer they would next try water torture.

The financial manager was an easygoing older man. He asked me how our experience had been, how were we treated, and a host of other questions, which amounted to a verbal quality control questionnaire. In a professional and blunt manner, I lambasted the entire process. "In 22 years of being involved in timesharing, owning seven weeks and going to at least 50 sales presentations, I have never been treated so poorly!" I gave him a summary of all that had transpired during the day. He feverishly took notes and shook his head.

"Rest assured, Mr. Paciello, these problems will be addressed. This is not the way this resort treats its guests. Please accept my heartfelt apology." "Finally," I thought, "a businessman who gets it, takes responsibility, and will implement corrective action." In the next instant, he shocked and amazed me. "Did the salespeople tell you about our special purchasing plan where you can own one week at the resort every four years? The price is incredibly low and could be an excellent asset to your timeshare portfolio." My brain went numb. I started to speak, but I couldn't get any air up into my throat. I menacingly leaned over the table. The manager slowly slithered his desk chair away from me. "Sorry folks, I'm required to offer you this final opportunity to purchase. Here is your check and your perks. Have a good day."

The logical question for considering purchasing timesharing vacations would be , if I could go back in time would I have purchased the weeks again? The answer is yes. However, the prospect of engaging in verbal combat during the sales presentations would damper my enthusiasm.

CHAPTER 7
Your New Dream House

You are probably receiving solicitations in the mail and reading advertisements in magazines inviting you to tour planned communities both traditional and retirement across the country. The offer is very similar to the timesharing introduction. They want you to visit their planned community. For a two or three day package at a much reduced rate ($59 to $149) plus perks (free golf, dinner, gift, etc.) most require a sales presentation. Some do not. This is a terrific way to have inexpensive vacations as well as getting a feel for both the location and type of community you may want to live in, either to own as a vacation home or the place you want to move to permanently. My wife and I have accepted this offer many times prior and during retirement. We have visited many properties throughout Florida, South Carolina, North Carolina, and Virginia. We identified these states as possible areas to make a permanent residence.

Of course, once you have decided to move to a warm weather climate, your next decision is to determine if you want to relocate to a planned community that is age restricted. Traditionally, one spouse had to be at least 55 years old, but that age requirement has become more liberal in recent years. Developers of adult communities are not stupid. They are targeting the Baby Boomer generation and that demographic will always ask the question, "What is the average age of the people living in the community? As the perspective home buyer, if you are, as an example, between the ages of 55-60, the chances are strong that you want to have neighbors who are similar in age. Living in an adult community is simply a matter of preference. In the recent annual Baby Boomer report by Del Webb, 59% of those surveyed planned to relocate for retirement. 7% of those planning to move, or approximately 2.4 million retiring Baby Boomers, are likely to consider an active adult community. With construction of adult communities on the rise, the percentage of retirees moving into these communities is likely to increase.

Planned communities that are not age restricted are attractive to home owners who want all the amenities of a private community, but are more comfortable living in a traditional setting. It's quite possible that the whole planned community concept is not for you. You don't play golf, tennis, or work out, have no interest in joining clubs, and have no desire to make new friends. In that case, why pay for amenities that you will not take advantage of?

The communities that we visited were all beautiful with indoor/outdoor pools, golf courses, health clubs, clubhouse, planned activities, etc. You get the sense that you could be on vacation 52 weeks a year. The nice part about these visits is there is rarely any pressure to sell you anything. Very few people are going to visit a property for the first time and plunk down a deposit fee for a new home.

You actually enjoy the sales presentation because you want to learn as much as possible about the home, the development, and the surrounding area. My most interesting experience with a planned community was a resort development in eastern Pennsylvania. Unfortunately, I never got to view the property.

This firm had been sending me invitations to view their

community for years. They offered nice gifts as an incentive, but because Pennsylvania was not on my target list to move, I declined. Finally, they hit my hot button! If you would preview their community, you were guaranteed a set of Tommy Armour irons. The resort was only two hours away. My wife and I could have a fun day trip. My irons were all beat up from playing bad golf. The only part of my clubs not abused was the sweet spot in the center of the clubface. My kids graduated Penn State. I liked Pennsylvania. I would be open-minded to see if Pennsylvania could be added to my housing list (By rationalizing the situation, I didn't feel guilty about accepting the free set of irons).

I called the number on the invitation. A young, bubbly woman answered. She was excited that I would be visiting. After asking me a number of pro forma questions, she wanted to confirm the date of the visit. I told her I would have to call her back and check with my wife (I was really calling to confirm that the free golf clubs had no strings attached). She assured me that everything was legitimate and even gave me all the specifications on the irons. I contacted my wife and confirmed a date to visit. I called the resort, but the person I spoke with was gone for the day.

The next day, my contact and I played telephone tag. Finally, we spoke that afternoon. As luck would have it, she could not find my paperwork and we had to start the application process all over again. We finished the process and she asked me to hold on for her supervisor who would confirm a couple of questions as a matter of procedure.

The supervisor got on the phone and instantly reminded me of Jack Webb of the old Dragnet TV series. She fired questions to me in a dry staccato cadence. She confirmed my marital status, that I had not visited the property previously, and a number of other questions that I had previously answered. She asked my occupation—I reaffirmed "retired". She asked, "What is your income?" Nothing, I live on my interest. "Your wife is a substitute teacher"? Yes. "What is her income"? "About $8,000, I replied." "I am sorry, sir, you don't qualify". "Excuse me?" I said in total befuddlement. She replied, "You must have a combined income of at least $50,000 to view our property.

I was caught between two emotions at the same time. On one hand, this is pretty funny. I am fortunate enough to retire at an early age and live off my interest (this was before the stock market crash when you did receive interest on your investments), and this lady is telling me that I don't qualify because the instructions say I must be employed and receiving a paycheck. This is hysterical. On the other hand, I am really ticked off for the very same reason. I am being rejected, treated like a leper because this firm has a boilerplate policy and the supervisor has no common sense.

I took a deep breath and tried to explain logically why her decision did not apply to me. I told her I appreciate the fact that the corporation doesn't want every Tom, Dick, and Harry visiting the resort and giving out free golf clubs to people who could not qualify to purchase a home. That makes perfect sense. However, if I am retired, have assets, and own my home outright; doesn't it make sense that I am the prototype person that you would want to have visit your property? Plus, I am in the middle of a search for a new residence and a very motivated buyer. The supervisor responded to my logic with a curt, "Sorry, sir, but according to our guidelines you don't qualify. If you would like to visit on your own without gifts or incentives feel free to do so. Good day." That day was one of the few times since I stopped working that retirement was a handicap instead of a blessing.

Let's assume that you were not treated like a leper when you instituted your new home search. You are ready to leave the cold and snow of the North and retire to your permanent new dream house in the Sun Belt. You have done your homework. You have visited a host of planned communities in different states. At last you have found the perfect home. Congratulations! But let's take a timeout. In my travels, I have been amazed at the disproportionate amount of time perspective home buyers spend deciding what model home they will choose and how they will decorate the house. It is fun and exciting to project yourself in your beautiful new home with all the wonderful amenities of the community, but this decision is really the final piece of the puzzle. It is far more important to do due diligence and confirm agreement in other parts of the process.

First, are you and your wife in total agreement? You may move to the Taj Mahal, but if one spouse isn't truly sold on it, you are setting yourself up for disaster. Have you made multiple visits to your new home at different times of the year? You may love Ocean City, Maryland in the summer with all the activity and hustle and bustle that is part of a seashore vacation community, but are you going to enjoy the solitude for nine months a year? On the other hand, you may have visited in the fall or spring and loved the community, but are you prepared for the summer rush and the bumper-to-bumper traffic that goes hand in hand with a popular resort destination? It is always a good idea to rent in off-seasons first before you purchase your home.

Next, make sure you understand all the fees and taxes that you are responsible for. Most prospective homebuyers feel they get a lot of house for the money in these warm weather communities, but many are motivated to move from home because of the high taxes. The real estate taxes in the new communities are usually very reasonable, but someone has to maintain the golf course, the health club, etc. When you add up the taxes and fees, the cost could be comparable with your current taxes. In my experience, the planned communities usually do an excellent job of highlighting and detailing all the expenses related to purchasing a new home.

Is living apart from your children and grandchildren going to be a problem? I have met a significant number of retirees who moved to warm weather climates, only to return home 3-5 years later to spend more time with their new grandchildren.

Is it a problem moving away from your friends? Everyone says they will visit, but in many cases it is not as simple as you may think. Are you and your wife social beings? Will you both make new friends easily? If you have a strong network of good friends and fortunately can transplant them over time into the same community in which you have purchased, you have struck gold. Personally, if I moved into a telephone booth, but had my friends close by, that would be far more important than discussing how we are going to design the guest bedroom.

Make sure that you are not only comfortable with your neighbors in the community, but what about your neighbors in the town? Is there a town? Many new developments are emerging in locations that are more rural and less developed. Is this your cup of tea, or will you be a fish out of water?

Make sure you are very clear on all the rules and regulations of the community you purchase in. What changes to your new home can you make? Can you build an addition? Planned retirement communities by definition may discourage you from having your grandchildren live with you for the summer and/or restrict their access to certain amenities on the property. Just make sure that you are aware of all the do's and don'ts before you sign on the dotted line.

Also, should you purchase in a new community that is just breaking ground, or purchase in a development that is established? Good question. In a new community looking to attract buyers, you are obviously going to get an attractive financial deal. However, you'll always have that fear factor that the developer will go bust and/or his timetable for completion of the project will be a myth. The penalty for getting in on the ground floor is years of construction, dirt, mud, etc., and not having the use of the planned amenities for a period of time. My advice is to do a lot of detective work. Check out the developer's track record, his funding, other communities that he has built, the Better Business Bureau, Chamber of Commerce, etc. Ask questions, assess your priorities within your timeframe, and make a decision.

There is a new trend that is building momentum in the development of planned communities. Age-restricted developments are springing up in the northeastern portions of the United States, as well as, in other cold winter areas across the country. This new concept fills the void for Baby Boomers who do not want to leave family and friends, but have no desire to shovel snow, cut grass, and walk up and down stairs. These home owners can participate in country club living and still migrate to the warm weather for an extended winter vacation. During the writing of this book, Florida got hit with an unprecedented four hurricanes in the same season. I suspect many retirees up north gave local retirement communities serious consideration.

I am reluctant to recommend any private communities, place to live, etc. My travel experience, while extensive, is primarily limited to the east coast of the United States to evaluate potential retirement destinations. The best resource for this information is a magazine aptly named *Where To Retire*.

The publication breaks down potential relocation venues and furnishes you with all the necessary statistics to help you make an informed decision. Category breakdowns include climate, humidity, rain, cost of living, median home price, applicable tax information, religion, education, transportation, health, and housing options. Of course the magazine is also filled with advertisements from developers trying to entice you to check out their properties.

That being said, I must comment on an active adult community that I visited which I felt was unique and yet very affordable for most people seeking a retirement development. The place is the Villages, located in The Villages, Florida. This is not a misprint! The development is actually its own self-contained town, with a population of about 60,000 people. When fully populated, the community will total about 100,000 residents. When you look for driving directions for an active adult community in your road atlas and see it listed on the map, you know that this place is different. Does size matter? Well, in the case of choosing a new retirement home, the answer is absolutely yes! Some people will not feel comfortable living in a development this expansive. Logistically, it takes a while to become comfortable with your surroundings. If living in solitude away from amenities and activities is your cup of tea, The Villages is not the place for you. I think a good analogy would be the time my children started visiting college campuses. My oldest son wanted to go to a small school, where student teacher ratios were attractive and you knew most of the people who attended the school. We didn't bother to visit any school that had a large student population. My two youngest children visited Penn State University. They saw the athletic facilities, the amenities on campus, and felt the buzz and energy that a major university has to offer, and decided on the spot that Penn State was the university that they wanted to attend.

Is The Villages the most desirable, coveted property that I have visited? No, not even close. Is the property on or located near the Gulf or Atlantic Ocean? No, it's located about one hour north of Disney World, in central Florida. Is The Villages located in a desirable, ascetically attractive area of Florida? No, I did not find the surrounding area particularly appealing. Then what is the attraction? The people that I spoke to on two separate visits to the Villages had one thing in common. They were happy! They described The Villages as the Disney World for adults. It offers every type of social club and sports participation that you can imagine. The amenities and recreation programs do not take a back seat to any of the more exclusive communities that I have visited. The Villages have twenty executive golf courses, all with various degrees of difficulty, and no cost to the residents! It offers eight championship golf courses with reasonable fees, and free membership to their country clubs. As noted before, The Villages is a sprawling complex, but it is broken down into many different neighborhoods, complete with their own amenities. The Villages now has two themed town squares which serve as the focal point for shopping, dining, and entertainment. Every night there is free live entertainment in the gazebo, and the residents are not shy about strutting their stuff. Their partying passion could be fueled by the fact that happy hour starts early in the afternoon and rotates to all the bars and restaurants in the town right through the early evening.

The homes in the complex are attractive and well-appointed. Most homes are priced between $150,000 and $500,000 and are built in a variety of sizes and models. One nice side benefit is that if a group of family and friends is interested in The Villages life style, there is a strong chance each family can purchase a home that fits its budget. I could go into more detail, but I am sure that you get my drift. The Villages can be reached at 1-800-245-1081, and on the web: www.TheVillages.com

CHAPTER 8
Cruising

I am hard pressed to find a better way to spend a vacation than by going on a cruise. When I was younger, cruising was expensive—a rich man's game. Boy, have times changed! The cruise lines have targeted the middle class to increase revenues and add more passengers to their vessels. Their marketing efforts have achieved great success over the past ten years, with an annual increase in cruisers of ten percent per year. Even with the high cost of oil and a slowing of new ships being launched which increased the cost of cruising about seven percent for 2005, the price per day of cruising is still ten percent lower than it was during 2001. In my opinion, not only is a cruise vacation the most enjoyable and comprehensive way to travel, but it offers you the best bang for your buck.

It seems that today the number of cruise destinations is endless. If a vessel can be docked in a body of water, then that city or town will make itself appealing to tourists. Utilizing the "if you build it, they will come philosophy," new ports of call are constantly being added to cruise line itineraries.

One striking difference in recent years is the number of themed cruises that are being offered. It wasn't that long ago that singles and senior cruises were the traditional alternatives to the generic cruise. Presently, if you are looking for a unique cruise, your options are overwhelming. You might want to go on a planned adventure cruise, or rub elbows with the rock stars or sports heroes of your youth. Why not toast your friends on a wine-themed cruise. You could even hang out (pardon the pun) with fellow nudists, and avoid the whole luggage hassle. If you are a real daredevil, you might want to contact a ship that combines these themes where you can drink wine naked in the Alaskan wilderness.

Since I have only taken four cruises during my retirement, all located in the Caribbean, I do not pretend to have an expertise in this area. However, I will shortly introduce you to two people who will recount their extensive cruise experiences. That being said, I must share with you a story that occurred on my first cruise.

My wife and I and our good friends Neil and Marcia Kasper sailed to the Eastern Caribbean for a seven day cruise. We had a wonderful time and the experience opened our eyes to the benefits and excitement of cruising. We visited Puerto Rico, Curacao, St Martaan, St Thomas, and Aruba. Being neophytes at cruising, my wife and I were extremely impressed with the level of service that the staff provided. The services provided ranged from cleaning your cabin and making up your bed whenever you disturbed it, to making sure that your every whim was accommodated in the dining room.

As is the case on most cruises, we had a young waiter who was assigned to our table for the length of the cruise. The young man was in his mid-twenties and of French and Lebanese extraction. He spoke English with a French accent which reminded me of Peter Sellers posing as French detective Clouseau in an old *Pink Panther* movie. Like most cruise staff, working on the ship was an opportunity to see the world and save some money for the future. Our waiter was personable and charming, but more importantly, he laughed at all of my corny jokes, even when he had no clue what I was talking about. He truly helped to make our cruise experience memorable.

Finally, the cruise was winding down, and we had our last dinner together. In the morning we would be homeward bound. Traditionally, this last supper is the time that you tip your waiter who has worked so hard to make your trip a success. The passengers presented their respective waiters with the gratuity envelopes. Hugs and kisses were exchanged. Even though you realize that you will never see this individual again, you somehow feel that you have made a friend for life. I waited for all the people at the table to say their final good byes. Before I presented the waiter with his gratuity, we had one of those genuine male-bonding moments. He told me that he never had so much fun with a passenger on a cruise. I countered with the fact that he is the best waiter that I have ever had on a cruise. I quickly reminded him that this was my first cruise and he has been the only waiter that I ever had. He laughed and told me that I am too much. I then proceed to give him an 8x12 photograph of himself flanked by my wife and me. The picture was taken earlier in the week by the ship photographer. He thanked me profusely. Then, I told him to turn over the picture and read my note on the back. This is what I had written.

Dear _____

Thank you so much for making this cruise such a wonderful experience for my wife and me. I wondered how I could show my appreciation for all that you have done during the week. I thought about giving you an extravagant tip, but I realized that the money would soon disappear, and you are probably the type of person who is not impressed with material gifts. In lieu of a cash tip, let me leave you with this picture of the three of us and the fond memories that we shared. Hopefully this photograph will be treasured by you and be in your possession for a long time.

Thanks,

Pat & Ethel Paciello

As he read the back of the picture, the blood drained from his face. He looked as if he were bitten in the neck by Count Dracula. He read the note a second time. His facial expressions made it easy for me to read his mind. "Are you kidding me? I busted my hump for this guy all week and he is going to stiff me?" I could not contain myself any longer. I burst into laughter and presented him with his well deserved tip. It took him a few seconds to realize that he was the victim of a practical joke. He fumbled for his words as he regained his breath and composure. "Oh, you got me, Mr. P—you got me good!" As my wife and I exited the dining room for the last time, I observed our waiter holding court with his fellow workers. He was extremely animated and was waiving his newly acquired photograph to any one within earshot.

However, more than just sharing my fond memories, I wanted to get a perspective on cruising from a travel consultant. I enlisted the services of the person who has booked my cruises and has successfully organized my travel plans. The following are Christine's responses to my questionnaire:

NAME: Christine Keefe

OCCUPATION: Travel Consultant

WORK HISTORY: 1997 to Present: Travel Consultant for Liberty Travel, Succasunna, New Jersey

WHAT HAS BEEN YOUR EXPERIENCE WHEN BOOKING CRUISES?

Booking a cruise is very frustrating for a travel agent.

When I book a cruise, everything is out of my control. It seems simple to the client. I just pick up the phone, get the rate and make the reservation. However, many of the cruise line reservationists are often incapable of truly helping the agent. I feel as an agent that it is my job to be knowledgeable about the product.

There are many cruise lines for the consumer to choose from and I have to find the right fit for the client, which requires knowing something about every cruise line. Often the reservationist simply does not know her own product. For example; I may have narrowed down a cruise to a seven day western Caribbean trip for a specific week. I then call the cruise line that will offer this trip but I may not know the specific ship. In my opinion, the reservationist should know off the top of her head which ships I have to choose from. She only has one cruise line to worry about. Unfortunately, it is usually quicker for me to fumble through the brochure than to wait for her to get back to me with the correct information. Frequently after the booking is complete, the cruise line confirmation fax has incorrect information on the ship, the date, the cabin category, or a misspelled name. If I don't double check the reservationist's work, I could end up with a huge problem for myself and my client.

In the final analysis, if my client has a problem due to an administrative foul up, it's my fault and my reputation.

WHAT IS THE DIFFERENCE IN CRUISE VACATIONS TODAY FROM THOSE IN THE PAST?

In today's cruise world there are more ships to choose from, and the ships are getting much larger. These new ships offer more balcony cabins, more dining options and more onboard activities for the family than ever before. If booked early, the cost of the cruise is usually more affordable than in the past. People assume that due to the size of these new ships, availability is not a problem. However, due to the attractive pricing structure, the demand has outstripped the supply. Thus the last minute bookers will pay a premium for their trip, and run the risk of being shut out.

IN GENERAL ARE CRUISERS SATISFIED WITH THEIR VACATIONS?

I try to contact clients after their trips to see if all went well. From their responses and their repeat business, I would have to say yes. Most of my clients who cruise, go year after year—they love it. I contacted a couple of my reps from different cruise lines to see what kind of statistical information they might be able to come up with on customer satisfaction. The average satisfaction rating was 93%, and the number of people who cruised more than once was approximately 80%. Royal Caribbean had an interesting fact. They maintain that 85% of the United States population has never taken a cruise. I'm not sure how they came up with that figure, but on the surface it seemed high.

WHAT CRUISE DESTINATIONS ARE THE MOST POPULAR, AND WHY?

Our clients, who are booking trips in the tri state area, seem to book mostly Caribbean cruises. I think the reason that these cruises are so popular for our clients may be that you can begin your vacation in a warm weather climate after a relatively short plane ride. Also, since 9/11, Alaskan cruises have supplanted European cruises for our clients who are not interested in the Caribbean.

IS THERE ANY ADVANTAGE TO BOOKING A CRUISE WITH A TRAVEL AGENT AS OPPOSED TO BOOKING A CRUISE ON THE INTERNET?

Clients seem to feel more at ease having their vacation

booked through an agent. If they have any problems or questions, they have a direct point of contact. The first-time cruiser may not understand the lingo of cruising. A travel agent has a lot (hopefully) of experience with different cruise lines and can try to match the needs of the client with the most suitable cruise line. Also, most trips booked online need to be paid in full at the time of booking. If the trip is booked outside the final payment period, (usually seventy one days prior to departure) we only require a deposit to confirm, and then the client can make payments as they please until the final payment is due.

Lastly, today the cost of a cruise is very competitive, whether you book a cruise directly with the cruise line, an internet service, or a travel agency. In the past, cruises could be purchased more inexpensively through a travel agent or via the internet because cruise lines did not have the manpower or the desire to oversee the sales process. Today the price of a cruise can usually be matched by the organization who covets your business.

CAN YOU COMMENT ON THE BEST CRUISE LINES AND / OR SHIPS AS IT PERTAINS TO SERVICE, VALUE, FOOD, AND ENTERTAINMENT?

Excluding the luxury cruise lines, such as Seabourn, Silversea and Crystal, I would rate Holland America as one of the top cruise lines for service and food. In general, Holland America tends to attract an older crowd. Celebrity is a close second and continues to get great ratings on their food and service. The Disney and Norwegian cruise lines are both known for their excellent entertainment, with Disney obviously catering more towards the family product. Royal Caribbean is another cruise line that offers good entertainment, along with extra activities for the family including a rock climbing wall, ice skating rink, inline skating, golf simulator, mini-golf and an excellent kids club. As far as value goes, it's really hit or miss. I would not say that one cruise line is always a good value or that one is always overpriced.

From my experience, I rate cruising to Bermuda to be a good value. One can depart from the New York / New Jersey area without making airline reservations. The ship serves as your hotel while you are in port, which means your meals and entertainment have been pre-paid (the cost of the cruise). Dining in Bermuda can be expensive, and the night life is not one of their selling points. The cruise ship can help fill that tiny void.

HAVE YOUR CLIENTS SHARED WITH YOU ANY UNUSUAL OR SIGNIFICANT EXPERIENCES ABOUT THEIR CRUISES?

The clients who booked a cruise so that they could ring in the new millennium found themselves in a unique situation. The cruise lines were taking deposits nearly five years in advance. The clients had no idea what ship, itinerary, or what the cost of the cruise would be. The deposit merely put you on a list to be notified before the cruises became available to the general public. A year and a half prior to the millennium, the cruise lines were able to give the clients more detailed information. However, the cruise lines could not guarantee that commercial air line flights could be booked. Eventually, the cruise lines enforced a stricter cancellation policy, and the cost of the millennium cruises were almost three times the amount of a comparable non-holiday cruise.

Due to the reasons cited above, every millennium cruise that was booked out of my office was cancelled, with the exception of one, who happened to be one of my clients. His millennium cruise was memorable for all the wrong reasons. Apparently, one of the crew jumped overboard during the night and committed suicide. When the ship realized the catastrophe, they had to turn around and search for the lost crewman. The passengers never made it to the port they were supposed to be in for their New Years celebration.

WHAT ADVICE CAN YOU GIVE TO PEOPLE WHO ARE CONSIDERING BOOKING A CRUISE?

Call me! Seriously, use a travel agent. If she is good, she will ask you a lot of questions and actually listen to the answers to help guide you toward the trip best suited for you and your family. A lot of times people come to the office and tell me that they want to book something specific. It's easy to be an order taker, but if I don't know them I try to find out why they chose this trip instead of something else. Sometimes people want to book something because someone they know did it and had fun, but that doesn't always mean they will. Everyone is unique. People have different goals and objectives for their cruise as well as varying budgets.

The last person to contribute input on cruising is a friend of mine, Frank Mugno. Frank is the Cal Ripken of cruising. In the last five years alone, Frank has embarked on over twenty cruises. I'm sure that by the time this book is published, Frank will be closing in on thirty cruises. In the spirit of Cal, Frank continues his unblemished and unbroken streak of consecutive cruises. I know of no other person who can provide such extensive personal experience on the subject. (When Frank takes his last cruise, does he jog around the outside of the ship waiving to the crew while they give him a well deserved standing ovation?)

In any event, the following is a brief background on Frank, and the events that led him to become the "cruise master."

Frank is a retired New York City police lieutenant. He served on the force for twenty-one years and retired at the age of forty-three. At the age of thirty-six, he purchased a home for investment purposes. For the next seven years he served two masters, as a police officer in the city and as an acquirer of real estate. Operating on very little sleep, Frank specialized in purchasing modestly priced homes, and then renovating them himself for sale and rent.

Frank had an epiphany after he had retired from the force. One of his best friends contracted colon cancer. He was only a year older than Frank and worked two and three jobs to support his family. His illness was slow and painful, and mercifully he passed away. This was a wake up call for Frank. He understood that there is more to life than making money. He proceeded to sell off most of his properties and explore the opportunities that retirement offered.

Frank's first major trip was a twelve day land tour of Italy, not a cruise. He enjoyed the trip and was bitten by the travel bug, but was not enamored with the daily bus rides from city to city and the constant packing and unpacking at the many hotels on the tour. He became convinced that most of the major cities in the world are located on oceans and rivers, and for him a cruise would be the best way to travel. The following are Frank's responses to the questions that I posed to him concerning cruising:

WHAT ARE SOME OF THE ENJOYABLE ASPECTS OF CRUISING?

When you travel by ship, you can enjoy the day time travel watching the scenery go by, utilize the many facilities of the ship, eat like there is no tomorrow, be very active, or do nothing at all. Your hotel room moves along with you. You go to sleep one night in one city and wake up the next day in another, refreshed, relaxed and ready to go! You have no worries concerning what clothing you should wear, what or where to eat, and the only time you pack an unpack your luggage is the first and last day of the cruise.

I love to cruise for two different reasons. One is for the sheer joy of cruising; the second is that cruising serves as a barometer to determine if I will return to a particular city for a longer stay. I enjoy meeting new and interesting people from all over the world. Cruisers are by their very nature well-traveled and it is a pleasure to exchange stories with them. My wife and I have made lasting friends from the people we have met on cruises.

The cruise ship itself offers a unique opportunity to develop new relationships. You get to know people over an extended period of time. Initially, you exchange the usual pleasantries, but as you see them day after day, you become friendlier, and over time you eventually loosen up. Before you know it, you are privy to their likes, dislikes, politics and some things that you don't need or want to know about them.

An example of how I utilized cruising to determine if I wanted to spend extended time in a city was a twelve day Baltic tour. The cruise began in London, England and ended in St. Petersburg, Russia. Along the way, we made one day stops in Helsinki, Stockholm, Estonia, Oslo, and Copenhagen. We were very impressed with London and St Petersburg, and at a later date we visited London for seven days, and signed on for a St Petersburg to Moscow river cruise down the Volga River for fourteen days. The river cruise was fabulous and educational. My past cruises have given me snapshots of potential cites to explore further, and I have repeatedly taken full advantage.

CAN YOU GIVE US AN OVERVIEW OF SOME OF YOUR CRUISE DESTINATIONS?

My first cruise was a Mediterranean voyage, which wetted my appetite for cruising. We have been to the Caribbean several times. We have cruised from San Diego to Miami through the Panama Canal, and visited the Baltics and Alaska. We cruised around the horn of South America from Buenos Aires, Argentina to Santiago, Chile, stopping along the way to see penguins in their natural habitat, and visited the Falkland Islands which the Argentines call Las Malvinas because they still believe that the islands belong to them. My wife and I took a river cruise down the Yangtze Sea River in China; we got to see the beauty of China before the river got completely flooded by the largest dam in the world.

We took two additional Mediterranean cruises, one from Venice to Barcelona to see the western Mediterranean, and one from Venice to Athens to view the eastern Mediterranean. This trip took in the Greek Isles which are spectacular, along with the Turkish cities of Kusadasi and Istanbul. Turkey is truly the cradle of civilization. My wife and I have also cruised the Mexican Rivera. This cruise starts in Los Angeles and proceeds down the West coast of Mexico to the cities of Cabo San Lucas, Acapulco, Xtapa, and Puerto Viarta. Wherever we have traveled in Mexico, the people were always warm and friendly. We journeyed to the Hawaiian Islands, an exotic location, but yet you are still on American soil. The cruise destinations that we have enjoyed the most spurred us to cruise them again, and as I mentioned previously, targeted those cities for land travel visits.

WHAT IS YOUR PHILOSOPHY ON CRUISING?

My philosophy is very simple. Find an itinerary that you like at the cheapest possible price. This will take time and effort, but it will be well worth it. I would rather take five or six inexpensive cruises a year rather than one lavish cruise. I subscribe to many news letters and internet travel sites. I receive all the "specials" and last minute bargains. Due to the fact that I am retired, I can mobilize quickly if a particular trip grabs my attention. Generally, I purchase an inside cabin. This is the most inexpensive way to cruise. Yet once you leave the cabin you have access to all the amenities of the ship. No one really cares if you are lodging in the penthouse suite or the boiler room. Also, inside cabins located on the lower decks are the most stable on the ship. The higher you reside on a ship, the more susceptible you are to high winds and rough seas. For me there is no motivation to take a cruise during holidays, weekends, school recess, Christmas breaks, or even summer vacation. The same cruise taken a week earlier or a week later will be less expensive, less crowded and more fun without a thousand screaming kids on board.

OF ALL THE CRUISES THAT YOU HAVE BEEN ON, WHAT IS YOUR FAVORITE?

I must say that my favorite cruises have been through the Mediterranean—hands down! The history and architecture in that part of the world is mind boggling. Where else in the world can you look at the Greek and Roman civilizations that date back thousands of years, see the natural beauty of Tuscany and Sorrento, marvel at the wonderful architecture of Barcelona and Monaco, and feel the uniqueness of Venice, all within a twelve day cruise? When you travel to that part of the world you soon realize that as Americans we really have a short history. There are huge edifices that were built hundreds of years before the first white man set foot in the new world. Until you go there and feel it for yourself, you can not appreciate the magnitude and scope of past history. Conversely, you get a better sense of how much we Americans have accomplished in a relatively short period of time.

WHAT ADVICE WOULD YOU GIVE TO FIRST TIME CRUISERS?

Different cruise ships cater to different clientele. Some ships cater to family oriented customers, others to the fifty-five plus audience, and of course some ships focus on singles cruises. For example, If you are a Baby Boomer who wants to relax, you probably do not want to be on a ship with thousands of screaming children. If you are a newlywed, it's usually more fun to engage with people of your own age, rather than on a ship filled with ancient mariners. If you choose a ship that doesn't match your profile, you run the risk of being turned off to cruising. The next item that I would consider is the length of the cruise. I would not recommend that a first time cruiser take a long cruise,—take one for five to seven days at most. Even with all the sea-sick medications available, you want to make sure that your system is not affected adversely by cruising. Although for most people, sea sickness is not a major concern. Next, take a cruise that is consistent with your vacation profile. If you like to bask in the sun and relax at the beach, then a Caribbean cruise is probably right for you. If you like to sight-see and be more active, then a Panama Canal or Alaskan cruise could be your cup of tea. After you have taken one or two cruises and have been bitten by the cruise bug like me, don't be afraid to sign on for more exotic ports of call.

WHAT ARE YOUR DOS AND DON'TS FOR CRUISING?

Do your homework before you book your cruise! As I stated earlier, I am logged into several cruise web sites, and receive newsletters which keep me abreast of the latest trends, prices, and last minute bargains on voyages all over the world. By doing due diligence, I am confident that I am picking the best cruise for the best price.

Once you arrive on the ship, take your time and do a walk-around. Familiarize yourself with the ship and where everything is located, especially on the new super vessels which are so big and intimidating that a novice could spend a significant amount of his time just trying to find the dining room. When you go to the dining room for lunch or dinner, make sure that you try new foods. Don't be afraid! If you don't like it, don't eat it! If you like three desserts, eat all three! Your waiter will be happy to accommodate your wishes. If you're looking to save a few dollars, don't order a can of coke for two dollars, order iced tea—it's free. This sounds insignificant, but if you are cruising with three or four soda-guzzling children on a seven to ten day cruise, then the savings could be significant. An added benefit would be that the children without their sugar rush would be able to fall asleep before the sun rises in the morning.

As far as gambling is concerned, my advice is to stay away. If you think it is tough to win money in Las Vegas, the casino on the cruise ship takes no prisoners. Save your money for the next cruise! While the price of cruising is very attractive, the opportunity to spend your hard-earned money on the ship is endless. From drinking, shopping, photographs, to shore excursions and everything in between, the ship is happy to accommodate your every whim, while they ring up the cash register.

Speaking of shore excursions—be selective! They are very expensive. If you take an organized shore excursion in every port of call, you can easily run up a bill of a thousand dollars or more. Most cruise destinations have cab drivers and tour guides waiting for you when you disembark from the ship. They are happy to drive you around and tour the area for a fraction of the cost of a ship sponsored excursion. However, if you are going to be on an all day excursion, far from the ship, I would recommend strongly that you take a ship sponsored tour. The ship will never leave port without one of their passengers if that passenger is on a ship authorized tour. If, however your taxi breaks down on the other side of the island and you are not on an authorized tour, and you don't make it back to the ship before the scheduled time of departure, your ship has sailed—literally and figuratively.

I saw this first hand for myself on a cruise to Nassau in the Bahamas. It was two o'clock in the morning in Nassau and we were ready to make sail back to New York. As the gang plank was being lifted, I noticed a cab speeding down the dock towards the ship. Two girls bolted out of the car, sprinting and screaming to the crew on the ship. The crew continued to raise the gang plank, and you guessed it, the girls were left on the dock as the ship sped away.

HAVE YOU HAD ANY UNUSUAL OR HUMOROUS CRUISE EXPERIENCE THAT YOU WOULD LIKE TO SHARE WITH THE READERS?

The first cruise that my wife and I took outside the United States provided a memorable experience. In May of 2000, we left for a twelve day cruise from Rome to Barcelona. Remember, this was prior to 9/11, and the travel restrictions that are standard operating procedure today were not implemented back then. The cruise's itinerary which commenced in Rome included daily stops in Sorrento, Malta, Athens, Livorno, the port city of Florence, Taormina in Sicily, and Monaco before reaching Barcelona. We arrived at JFK Airport three hours before our scheduled flight with ten—I repeat ten—suitcases! My wife had filled eight suitcases and I laid claim to the other two. We were pushing two large luggage carriers around the airport to check our luggage. At the check-in counter, the attendant told us we had too much luggage. He asked us what pieces were we going to leave behind? Our answer was simple—"none." The clerk decided that he would check our luggage but it would cost us an additional seven hundred and twenty dollars. I refused his offer. Now a full-fledged debate was being waged between the clerk and me. The longer the debate, the longer the check in line was swelling behind me. He counter—offered me with an additional fee of three hundred and sixty dollars. I promptly refused. Other travelers in awe of our excessive luggage, started taking our pictures. We had become the first tourist attraction of the cruise. Ten minutes later, the attendant cut the fee in half again, to one hundred and eighty dollars. I declined, and the line continued to grow. The people behind me on line were getting a little testy and they screamed at the counter man to process us through. He made a new proposal for ninety dollars, which was quickly rejected by me. Finally, he waved the white flag of surrender, threw his hand up in the air and said, "I give up." He tagged the entire luggage and sent it through at no additional cost. The crowd started to cheer and off we went to begin our flight to Rome.

When we arrived at the cruise ship in Rome, we had no problem checking our excessive luggage. The cruise ships at the time had no restrictions on the amount of luggage you could bring onto the ship. This, however, is not the end of the story. Once we entered our tiny cabin with our ten suitcases, it was a logistical nightmare. I was absolutely amazed when my wife started to empty out the contents of her suitcases. She had packed thirty pairs of shoes. Imelda Marcos had nothing on my wife. As the cruise was winding down, I asked myself how the heck I was going to get all this luggage back on the airplane? Due to my wife's penchant for shopping, the luggage was expanding at an abnormal rate. What if the check-in people in the Rome airport played hardball on the luggage issue? My wife assured me that she would solve our problem. This was her solution. After scanning all the check-in line clerks in the airport, she got on the luggage check-in line of the clerk who had the most sympathetic face. I feigned being nasty and mean to my wife in front of the clerk. I then walked away from my wife in a huff. My wife then approached the clerk and said, "I know that I have too many pieces of luggage, but I could not help myself. I bought every thing in sight from your beautiful country. My husband is so angry I think he is going to kill me. I don't know what to do." As my wife revealed this sob story to the clerk, the clerk clutched her chest and in her best broken English cried out, "I know the heart of a woman," and proceeded to tag all twelve bags of luggage. She then turned and glared at me and then gazed back at my wife and said,"Bastard!" That one word saved me a lot of money and aggravation. We never over-packed on a cruise again!

CHAPTER 9
Financial Strategy

The first question most Baby Boomers ask as they close in on retirement is how much money they need to have accumulated to be able to walk away from their jobs and go into retirement mode. Unfortunately, the answer is not generic and is based on a variety of factors which include psychological and emotional, as well as financial issues. The first thing that you want to do is to fill out a retirement profile, and utilize a financial online calculator that will list your assets and income streams (pensions, social security), versus your expenditures when and if you retire. You can calculate how long your money will last based on various interest rates and prevailing inflation rates that you will be accruing on your principal and what, if any, shortfalls will occur during the course of retirement. These tools are freely available on the Internet, included in financial magazines, and are utilized by brokerage houses as a marketing tool to get you to invest your money with them. The information obtained is not the be all and end all to your financial query, but rather a first step to getting you organized and giving you a glimpse of what the future holds for you.

Presently, the most innovative web-based tool to assist you with your retirement planning is Fidelity's Retirement Income Planner. RIP, as it is known as, is very helpful for retirees who want to get a better handle on how they can live off their investments. Walter Updegrave, a senior editor for Money magazine wrote an excellent article outlining the benefits and features of RIP, which peaked my interest. Once you enter your financial data, you will get immediate feedback on how many years your investment nest egg will be able to cover your living expenses. The next step is to mix and match a variety of "what if" scenarios, such as whether to delay Social Security benefits, reduce living expenses, work part time, change your portfolio asset strategy, etc, to get a clearer understanding of what you need to do for the future to achieve your financial goals. Mr. Updegrave points out in his article that other major financial service firms are poised to unveil their competing products in the near future. High tech, interactive financial planning will become the standard for Baby Boomer retirees.

I would be remiss in this chapter, if I did not comment on Social Security, a topic which gathers increasing importance as we march on to retirement age. Here is a quick tip on how important your Social Security check will be for your retirement. If you spend more than two minutes studying your semi-annual projected Social Security statement, you have not saved enough to retire. Allen Greenspan, the former Federal Reserve Board Chairman, has echoed a familiar refrain to Congress, one that he has repeated a number of times during 2004. His message is simple. Social Security and Medicare benefits must be recalibrated, so that Baby Boomers can have a realistic idea of what to expect from these programs when they retire. Nobody is refuting the facts. The Congressional Budget Office predicts that Social Security left in its present state will go bust in 2052. Medicare could be insolvent by 2019. By the year 2025 Social Security will have only 2.25 workers supporting each retiree.

President Bush recently laid out his plan to revamp

the Social Security System. I must confess that I am totally confused by the venomous reaction of some to his proposal. Republicans and Democrats have long been in agreement that the system is in need of repair. Yet, the first time that someone moves from the *let's form another subcommittee and continue to talk about the situation,* to *let's solve the problem and take some action,* he is portrayed as the grinch that stole Social Security. The Social Security System repair should be motivated by economic, not political motives. You may agree or disagree with the President's proposed changes, but let's evaluate the plan logically on the merit of the proposal, and let's hear opponents of the plan offer their solution to the problem.

The part of the President's plan that gets all the media coverage and fans the fire of discontent of his opponents is the ability of participants to invest over time four percent of payroll taxes in a personal retirement account. Now, unless I am missing something, the plan is voluntary. You don't have to participate if you don't want to. If you choose to invest in a personal retirement account, the amount of payroll taxes at risk in the private sector is relatively low, with the opportunity to earn a better rate of return. What's the problem? The message from people who are adamantly opposed to any form of private investing of our payroll tax is clear. We don't trust people to invest their own money. Let the government manage your money. Well, no thanks. If the government were doing such a wonderful job managing the Social Security fund, we wouldn't need to fix it.

Anyway, the private accounts debate makes for a nice sound bite on television, but it really is a peripheral issue. The only question that really matters is how we are going to realistically fund future generations' retirement. Unless we develop new or divert existing tax dollars, the future of Social

Security seems pretty obvious to me. No politician who wants to remain in elected office is going to vote to dismantle Social Security. However, it is just as certain that the age requirements for eligibility, and probably benefit payments, are going to be adjusted, and not in your favor. But look at the bright side. As parents, we will be helping to lift a financial burden from our children. I can't imagine the government cutting benefits to people already receiving them, and they are going to tread lightly with people who are close to retirement age. If receiving benefits is important to augment your financial strategy, you might be advised to opt for partial benefits commencing at an earlier age. This way, you lock yourself in as a Social Security recipient.

Of course, for most of us, calculating our retirement strategy is a reflection on what we have earned and saved during our working careers. If you have not built up a nice nest egg for retirement and/or have pensions or other income streams to tap into, realistically, retirement is probably a myth. Stop sticking pins in that doll that looks like your boss, and figure out how you can increase your assets and lower your cost of living. There are many good books written in detail on how to acquire wealth, save money, and invest successfully. That is not the focus of this book. Hopefully, as Baby Boomers you have made the right financial decisions to allow yourselves to contemplate retirement. However, for the sake of our children, let me pass on to you the wisdom of Baby Boomers who are retired or plan to be retired soon. The following are the secret and insightful thoughts of the best of our generation:

The Top 10 Strategies to Retire Early

1. Have rich parents
2. Make sure your rich parents name you as beneficiary in their Will

3. Hit the lottery
4. Win a frivolous law suit and settle for a huge cash settlement
5. Start a new company that is wildly successful
6. Work for a new company that is wildly successful, which gives you stock options
7. Become a teacher
8. Marry a teacher
9. Become a rock star
10. Become a professional athlete

Most of these strategies require either a lot of luck or a unique ability. How does becoming a teacher make the top 10 list? By teachers, I am really including anyone that is represented by a strong labor union and working in the public sector, a union that not only negotiates a competitive compensation package but has extremely good retirement benefits. In my travels, when I met Boomers who had retired early, a significant percentage of these people were teachers, policemen, and firemen. My point is not to debate whether these professions are overpaid or underpaid, or to examine the risk, stress, or job satisfaction associated with the job, but rather to simplistically demonstrate how these career paths can lead to a very pleasant early retirement. I will profile the teaching profession to illustrate my point.

Every school district in New Jersey has its own compensation package for the teachers that it employs. However, the districts are fairly uniform in the methodology they utilize to determine salary and benefits, and what they actually offer has to be somewhat competitive or all the quality teachers of one district would flock to the neighboring town that offered them a significantly better pay and retirement program.

Let's assume we have a hypothetical couple who graduate college, become teachers and then get married. They both retire after working 33 years, having earned their Masters degrees and acquiring 30 additional credits. This continuing education not only serves them well in their vocation, but also increases their base salary. At 55 years of age they are each making about $80,000. A teacher's pension is based on the average salary of his last 3 years of employment. The formula that is utilized to compute the pension is the number of years that one had worked divided by 55. In this case 33/55 equals 60% of $80,000 or $48,000. Multiply this by 2 pensions and you have a family pension for life of $96,000.

However, the pension is not the best part of the retirement package. Once you have worked for 25 years for the school system, you receive lifetime medical benefits, plus your pension increases in response to the Cost of Living Index. This windfall does not include monthly Social Security checks for the couple or any additional savings or investments they may have accumulated over the years. In addition, once a teacher has attained tenure, his job security ranks just behind death and taxes as an absolute certainty, and we have not even mentioned summer vacation. Adam Sandler might say, "It ain't too shabby!"

Now compare and contrast a teacher with friends and neighbors who work for corporate America. Many qualified individuals have been laid off from their jobs. The ones who are lucky enough to hold on to their positions, work under the threat of dismissal and are asked to work more hours, usually for less pay. Benefit programs have been slashed and pension and retirement funds have been eroded, thanks to a slumping stock market.

The value of the lifetime health benefits is an enormous

retirement perk for a teacher. As a retiree with no subsided health plan, the cost for my monthly heath insurance coverage is approximately $900 per month for 2 adults and no children. The plan is an HMO, with $30.00 copay, and I pay 50% of the retail cost for my prescriptions. Many Baby Boomers will be forced to delay their retirement, not because of lack of savings and investments, but because of the rude awaking that health care costs will become a significant financial burden.

Do I sound jealous? (Sorry, I was trying to conceal that from you.) If you are like me you already have some sense that teachers and other individuals represented by influential unions have pretty good retirement benefits, but when you read the information on the printed page it makes a powerful statement. My friend Georgia Grant, a teacher for 29 years in the local school system, likens the teaching profession to the old tale of the tortoise and the hare. Teachers often start their careers slowly compared to other professions, but they seem to get to the finish line first and in better financial shape than most.

But what if your child has no interest in becoming part of academia? Maybe your child has no desire to attend college. No problem. The public sector is not only willing to employ him but will do it's best to provide substantial retirement benefits. If you are one of the chosen few, you could land a job with the New Jersey Department of Transportation and become a toll taker working in a booth on one of our many congested highways. The benefits are excellent and the last time a toll taker was put in harm's way was in *The Godfather*, when Sonny got whacked. However, you must accept the fact that your left arm will always be tan, while your right arm will be pale due to lack of sunlight.

Lastly, you can't have a discussion about retirement

plans and omit the men in blue. Policemen have outstanding benefits that can rival any profession. I won't bore you with the statistics, but even the teachers are envious. Many police officers with overtime make more money than the District Attorneys who prosecute their arrests. The good news here is that lawyers are aware of this potential inequity and some are abandoning their professions to become policemen. If this trend gains momentum, our streets will have more cops and fewer lawyers.

My advice to you? When you can't beat them, join them! When your kids and your grandchildren are ready to enter the work force, if they have an interest in working for the public sector, don't discourage them. Many of us would like to see our children become CEO's of large corporations, like WorldCom or Tyco. Ah, scratch that, bad examples. But the reality is that working for the public sector supported by an aggressive union can offer a productive career and a quality retirement. When friends who worked for corporate America complain about their meager pensions and poor but expensive health coverage, you can feign empathy knowing that your offspring's future is well protected. Willy Nelson recorded a song, "Mammas Don't Let Your Babies Grow up To Be Cowboys." He was right. In my travels, I have not met a single Baby Boomer Cowboy who has retired. You know why they sleep on the open range and eat beans every night huddled around a campfire? They have no retirement benefits! Trust me. Let your babies grow up to be teachers.

The good news and bad news for Boomers considering retirement is that we are statistically going to live longer than our parents. The bad news is that we are going to live longer than our parents and will need more money to fund our retirement. If you fill out your worksheet and your time frame for retirement is approaching, this can be a sobering experience. If you have started the planning for retirement earlier, 10 to 15 years before you plan to leave the workforce, you have time to make adjustments so that you can accomplish your financial goals. Of course, you can flush the worksheet down the toilet and announce to your children that they will have the burden of caring for you in retirement. After all, it's only fair. You provided for them for all of their lives and asked nothing in return. It's time for the kids to step up to the plate and take care of mom and dad in their golden years. Once they stop laughing, you can eliminate this retirement strategy. Another possible scenario could be living well above your means in living "La Vida Loca" retirement until your money dries up and then you simply expire when your last dollar was spent. This process would insure that no one would bear the burden and responsibility for caring for you in your latter years. Although this sounds ghoulish, you could have some fun with this scenario. Should you go out with one big mega party or possibly stage your own lavish wake? You could host it and watch and listen to your friends swap stories about what a great guy you were. The decision-making process alone should keep your mind sharp. However, this radical approach is frowned upon in our society and probably has little practical application.

Once you have a pretty good handle on your financial picture, you have to make lifestyle decisions. Do you want to start a new career? Do you want to work part-time? According to the Baby Boomer Report done annually by Del Webb since 1996, those surveyed felt that they would need more than $800,000 in retirement savings and expected it to last them for nineteen years. The April 2003 survey showed that 43% of Baby Boomers ages 44-56 plan to continue work. 76% of the Boomers surveyed are not confident that they have saved enough money for retirement. When I read this report, what jumped out at me was that 76% of the people felt that they didn't save enough for retirement, yet only 43% planned to continue to work. That leaves 33% who don't feel they have saved enough, but still don't plan to work.

My take on the situation is that if you have the opportunity to retire early or even take a sabbatical for a period of time, do it. You can preview retirement, try new careers or jobs or do nothing at all. You may find that not working makes you miserable. For me, the last five years have been fun. Fortunately, I am blessed with the ability to do nothing and yet do it well. I wouldn't trade the memories for the compensation that I could have earned. If you have your health today, you may not have it tomorrow. Activities that you cherish today may not be as important to you tomorrow. We have all heard stories or know of people who work their whole lives to build an impressive nest egg. They finally feel they are financially ready to retire in style and then get sick or pass away. I have a feeling that when I am older I will look forward to the opportunity to rejoin the workforce. I certainly will be well rested.

What kind of lifestyle do you want to live in retirement? Do you want to maintain your present lifestyle or are you willing to do with less so that you can walk away from your current job? Once you decide to retire, you have to decide how you are going to invest your money. After filling out your worksheet, you will probably need to earn some percentage of interest each year to protect your principal and keep up with inflation. As in all investing, you have to decide how much risk you are willing to take to potentially maximize your reward. The key here is not to get greedy. If you need to earn $75,000 a year from your investments, use an investment strategy that gives you the best opportunity to reach this goal with the least amount of risk.

I had about $1.5 million to use as my retirement fund. Most of this money; came from the sale of my business. On one hand, to many people this seems like a large sum of money, but when you stop working at 50 years of age and estimate that you may live another 35 years, your wife has a part-time job that nets less than $10,000 and you still have two kids in college, it's not really a lot of money to live the rest of your life on. My strategy was to invest the entire amount in the stock market. Math is not my strong suit, but even I could figure out that at 10 or 11%, the historic average gain of the stock market, I could fund my retirement with the interest I would accumulate. I knew putting all my money in the stock market was risky, but if I didn't get at least a 10% return, my retirement plans would have to be adjusted. Plus, the stock market was percolating through the late 90's, and a 10% return on my money would actually be disappointing.

I could invest my money in one of the following ways:

(a) Day trader—I had friends who were managing their own portfolios. As the stock market skyrocketed, especially tech stocks, they fancied themselves as the next Warren Buffet. While most of these people were making impressive returns, it was obvious this was a full-time job. You had to be near a computer and a phone at all times. You either possessed a neurotic personality, or day-trading your own portfolio would make sure you became crazy. This method was definitely not for me.

(b) Index funds—In this case, invest in a fund that mirrors the S&P 500 (Blue chip, large cap growth funds). The expenses and costs of running this type of fund are very low. Vanguards fund had a very impressive track record. Its lower expenses resulted in a better rate of return than its peers. I gave strong consideration to this strategy.

(c) Stockbroker—I had mixed feelings about using a traditional brokerage firm. On one hand, I wanted to have a professional broker to whom I could have access immediately and solicit advice. On the other hand, nobody cares more about your own money more than you do, and a stockbroker makes his money by selling you products and executing trades. A successful broker is not only financially astute, but he is a good salesman.

(d) Financial planner—In this case, a fee-based firm or individual who would charge a yearly fee to put your financial portfolio in order.

As I was debating which was the best vehicle to invest my money in, I saw an advertisement in the local paper. The ad offered a series of basically free retirement seminars. A registration fee of $49.00 to cover the cost of materials was the only charge. You were required to attend one seminar per week for four weeks. The course would cover all the financial aspects of retirement with multiple topics being featured every week. When the course was finished, if you chose, you would receive your own personalized financial report with the investment firm's recommendations. The program was titled Financial Strategies For Successful Retirement offered by Smith Barney. They emphasized there would be absolutely no soliciting of you to become a client. This advertisement was exactly what I was looking for. Like most people, I could not claim to have any real financial or investing experience. My knowledge of these subjects as it related to retirement planning was zero. By participating in the program, I could educate myself on various areas of retirement planning; and if I decided not to use Smith Barney as my investment advisor, which at the time seemed probable, I wouldn't feel obligated or guilty.

The course was directed by Mort and Alan Reisfeld, a father and son team. Mort was in his sixties and possessed a tremendous zeal for his work. He reminded me of Henny Youngman with his corny, but infectious humor. His son Alan came across more serious and played the straight man, wisely letting his dad be the star of the show. The retirement seminars were excellent. Different speakers were introduced to the group to lecture on their particular area of expertise (estate planners, insurance specialists, etc). Everyone who participated received a loose-leaf book filled with the seminar topics and other materials. At the end of the course, all the attendees received a nice-looking individualized managed assets report, which was based on the information that the attendees provided to the Reisfields. Smith Barney would devise a financial strategy that was tailored to your financial objectives. Now, truth be told, the information in both manuals was very generic in nature. The individual managed assets report probably didn't vary all that much from person to person. I don't think there were too many people in the retirement program that checked the box that read, "I want high volatility and high risk to achieve maximum returns."

As much as I was participating in the seminars to become knowledgeable about retirement strategies, I was evaluating Mort and Alan to determine if I was going to tab them to invest the money that I received from the sale of my company. I was waiting for them to subtly make their sales pitch on why Smith Barney was the best choice to invest my money. To my pleasant surprise, as advertised, there was no sales pitch and no pressure exerted to utilize their services.

As a businessman, I thought to myself, this is an excellent marketing concept. While certainly not unique, it definitely was effective and extremely well executed. You spend one night a week for 4 weeks with people who want to manage your money. You are participating in these meetings because you are at the first stage of planning your financial strategies for retirement. You obviously do not have a firm that you are 100% comfortable with acting as your financial advisor. You are a captive audience. If the seminars go well and you develop a level of trust with Mort and Alan, the odds are that you will utilize their services. Following the same theory, Mort and Alan brought in guest speakers who were eager to volunteer their time for the opportunity to market their services to a targeted audience.

In the final analysis, I decided to utilize Smith Barney. I am not really convinced that once you decide to go with a large brokerage firm there really is all that much difference from one firm to the other. They all market similar products and their rates are similar. I went with Smith Barney because Mort and Alan gave me a level of confidence and trust. They were sincere and honest. They gave me the impression that they would safeguard my finances.

After the ringing endorsement, I am happy to say that Mort and Alan still represent my financial interests today, but the road has not always been smooth and the volatile stock market of the new millennium tested the best business relationships.

Once I decided to have Alan and Mort direct my portfolio, my financial strategy was a simple one. Some would say naïve. I wanted to invest in blue chip growth companies only, Fortune

500 brand name corporations, the IBM and Microsoft's of the world. To achieve my financial objectives and not have to go back to work, I would need to get the 11% return the stock market historically produced. If I watered down my investment strategy and included bonds and cash into my portfolio, I would reduce my risk, but would not be able to get the return I needed in my investments. I thought my approach was actually pretty conservative. The stock market was heating up and it seemed everyone was making 20% plus in their investments no matter what they invested in.

When I relayed this information to Allen, he suggested that I focus my investments more in value-oriented funds and less in growth. He demonstrated that value-oriented firms (quality firms that are thought to be under-valued by the portfolio manager and thus can be purchased at reasonable prices) have historically outperformed growth companies. Alan divided my money into three different managed funds: Oppenheimer Value Portfolio, Rittenhouse Core Portfolio and Boston Safe Advisors Large Cap Value Equity. He demonstrated the past performances of these funds and the track record of the portfolio managers. He utilized a variety of charts demonstrating the volatility of the funds and their risk/return analysis. In short, Allen did due diligence and educated me on this investment strategy. The fee for utilizing Smith Barney to manage my portfolio was about 1% of the amount I had invested with them. This fee was deducted from the portfolio on a quarterly basis. I liked the fact that I never had to write out a separate check for the service and the portfolio managers had no incentive to churn the account—buy and sell stocks to increase brokerage fees.

What happens next is a matter of history. The blue chip stocks soar and the tech stocks go off the charts. The only investor who is unhappy is the value investor. Your friends who have no clue on how to invest in the stock market are making 40, 50% plus return on their money. Meanwhile, I am supported by this sophisticated financial team and I am making about 7% on my money. It's difficult, but I continue with the stay-the-course investing strategy, changing funds, but not my value strategy. This proves to be a bad mistake. I miss out on the financial gold mine of the late 90's. Allen is having a rebellion from his value clients, and investors are ready to find another firm to represent them. For self-preservation, Allen relents from his conservative investment approach. He calls me up and suggests that I hop onboard the tech stock bandwagon and put a portion of my money into a fund that owns profitable companies on the NASDAQ Exchange. I complied, and six months later the stock market crashed and burned.

Now, just about everybody was impacted with the stock market decline and the ensuing economic recession. The more money that you put at risk, the greater the devastation. Baby Boomers probably were devastated more than any other group. We had the money to invest and saw the stock market as our highway to fund our retirement. When you are in your 40's and 50's, it is a lot more difficult to pick up the pieces from faulty financial decisions than it is when you are in your twenties and thirties. Most people I talked to who were over 60 years old were not seduced by the surging stock market, and those who invested, invested what they could afford to lose.

Like most unpleasant experiences, there are lessons to be learned. Based on my investing track record, I now have the wisdom of Solomon. The following are my thoughts about investing.

(a) It's your money. Take an active role in your investment strategy; but you do not want to manage your own portfolio, meaning buying and selling stocks, a.k.a. day trading, unless you have an investment expertise and enjoy doing this as a second career. But you do not want to be one of those people, and there are many, who blindly turn over their money to a third party. They have only a vague idea about the companies they are investing in and have no real clue on how to evaluate the funds or the financial advisor, as well as the costs, including fees and commissions. These same people will haggle over the price of a straw hat at a flea market, but are very passive when entrusting their retirement nest egg to investment professionals.

(b) Having a financial professional to advise and educate you is definitely helpful in plotting your financial strategy. That being said, finding an honest, sharp, trustworthy person is paramount. Multiple convictions on fraud and embezzlement highlighted on the firm's promotional literature are usually a dead giveaway to avoid this kind of advisor. Any financial consultant who is going to create wealth for you by selling and trading individual stocks should be avoided at all costs. He is a salesman, makes money on individual trades, and probably has no more experience in the financial area than you do.

(c) Diversify your portfolio to reduce risk. This means both the diversification of your assets, stocks and bonds, cash, and don't forget real estate. Most Baby Boomers regret they didn't delve into the real estate market more heavily. Real estate opens up a revenue stream independent of the stock market. In your stock portfolio, diversify your companies to include a mixture of strategies: growth, value, large cap, overseas investing, etc. Mutual funds are the easiest way to accomplish this objective. And certainly do not rule out Index funds or funds that mirror Indices: Standard and Poors, Dow Jones, and NASDAQ, as part of your portfolio.

(d) Measure the performance of your portfolio against the corresponding bench markets. If you have a fund that is made up of large cap funds, you compare the fund's performance versus the S&P and more importantly, the Lipper or Morningstar ranking of mutual funds broken down into their various investment strategies. If the S&P has returned 22%, your fund has a return of 17% and is ranked in the bottom third of funds in its category, your fund has done a poor job. You would have been better off buying an Index, Spider or Diamond fund that closely mirrors the S&P, incurring fewer costs including commissions, expenses, and fees.

The attitude of most investors, sadly, is that if they are making a good rate of return (double digits), they are content and will be satisfied with the status quo. They may moan and groan, but push come to shove, they will keep the financial advisor who put them into the fund and probably continue with the fund as part of their portfolio.

Let's say that you have invested in a fund that consists of mid-cap value companies. You compare the performance of your fund to the Russell 2000 Value Index. Your fund has lost 6% of its value, while the Russell 2000 Value Index has lost 10% of its value during the course of the year and is ranked in the top 1/3 of funds in its category. Your fund has done a terrific job. The portfolio manager should be congratulated.

Of course, most investors don't feel that way. They have less money at the end of the year than they had at the beginning. Heck, they could have put their money in the bank and made a positive return on their money with no risk. The investor is out for blood and heads will roll. You might want to alter your investment strategy and put your money into a different investment sector. The truth is that you have a fund that is outperforming its peers and when the sector turns around, the chances are strong that it will outpace the other companies in its categories.

One of my pet peeves when investing money with a managed asset program is paying 1-2% to the investment firm to manage your assets. I have no problem paying the fee. The brokerage firm doesn't work for free. However, I feel the system is in need of a face-lift. For example, let's assume you have $1,000,000 invested and your fee is 1%. At the end of the year, assuming your assets didn't change, you would pay $10,000 to the firm for managing your money. Let's assume the portfolio manager had a great year and not only increased your portfolio by $300,000 (30%), but beat the comparable indices and was ranked in the top 10% of the funds in its category. At the end of the year, your fee for his services would be 1% of 1.3 million dollars or $13,000. I think not only should that manager get a thunderous round of applause and possibly my first male child, but also he should participate and be rewarded greater for his fine performance. It cost me only $3,000 more in commission to achieve $300,000 more in assets than the prior example, which yielded no return. Let's look at a more unpleasant scenario. The portfolio manager does a miserable job. He loses 30% of your assets and no matter which yard stick you measure his performance by, the result stinks. Your assets have now been reduced to $700,000 and you must look at your year-end summary and be reminded that you paid your investment firm $7,000 to have your money legally pick-pocketed. Should you reward an investment firm for such poor performance? Instead of the investment house apologizing and extending mea culpas, it should return the fee back into the portfolio. Share the financial pain with the client. I guarantee this system will upgrade the performance of brokers and portfolio managers and weed out of the industry those whose skills should be utilized in other professions.

CHAPTER 10
Parents/Children

As a retired Boomer, the relationships with your children and your parents take new twists and turns. Somebody once said, "You can retire from your job, but you never retire from life." That statement is absolutely true when it pertains to your children and your parents. Many Boomers naively view retirement as a simple economic plan. "I need x amount of dollars for my retirement. Once I have amassed the money that I need, I will quit my job, begin my life of leisure and sail off into the sunset." Now, we know that life doesn't work that way, and most of us have the scars and bruises that are inevitable as we make the journey into retirement. As parents, our children's odysseys have or will have their own unique stories. That being said let me outline a generic timeline that is all too common for most parents. You probably can identify with some, but hopefully not all of the various stages.

1...You save enough money or borrow enough money to send your children to college.

2...They graduate and can not find employment in their chosen field.

3...They move back home.

4...They talk about moving out, but the free room and board, plus the many concierge services that their mother provides, makes living with their parents tolerable.

5...They eventually find a good job, and move out.

6...They get married.

7...You feel bad that they are living in a small apartment, so you lend them money for a down payment for a house.

8...They divorce.

9...They move back home.

10...Maybe the failed marriage has produced grandchildren. As grandparents, we take an active role in babysitting and child care so that our son or daughter can find a good job and....

I know that I am painting a bleak scenario, but do not despair. The first day that your children are leaving the house at 6:30 to fight bumper to bumper traffic to get to work, when you are happily retired and sleeping soundly, that my fellow Boomers, as the MasterCard commercial decrees, is truly priceless!

Your life as a parent who has retired from his job never goes as you had imagined. Let's use an example that we all can identify with, automobile insurance. You have retired and your son has graduated from college and is working in the real world. You think, at last, I can take my child off my insurance policy, reduce my premiums significantly and eliminate the risk of having a young driver on the policy. Then you remember that even though you do not drive your son's car, you are the registered owner of the car. (Car dealerships are not big fans of providing auto financing to young unemployed drivers). It has become your responsibility to contact the insurance company. Your son has no motivation to get his own insurance. He is very happy to continue with the status quo. After all, how sympathetic is the insurance firm going to be when your son claims poverty and promises to pay double the following month. It's going to be far more difficult to sweet talk the company than it is your father.

You call the insurance firm to get your child off your policy and inquire what the cost will be for his new policy. The agent gives you the price quote. Realizing that he has made a foolish error, you laugh and explain to the agent that you are not looking to purchase a car, but are seeking basic auto insurance for your child. He confirms the premium, an amount so staggering that you lose your ability to speak. "How is this possible?" you inquire when you recover from your temporary stroke. The agent feels your pain. I am sure that he has had this conversation on numerous occasions with policy holders. He empathetically explains the reasons why the premiums are akin to a king's ransom. He does have good news though. He has just saved a bundle of money on his car insurance. (Sorry, I couldn't resist). He explains to me, that when my son turns 25 years old, his premiums will be lower. How much will the premiums fall? Nobody knows. This is one of life's greatest mysteries. However one thing is certain. If your child should get a traffic violation or get into a car accident, he will be branded deeper than a steer on the Ponderosa. Even the Cartwrights won't be able to save him. Once you realize that your child could never afford to pay these exorbitant premiums, you try to mix and match every possible combination of driver and vehicle to lower your insurance bill. In the end you realize that you are doomed. You relent and do the fatherly thing. You go back to square one and continue to have your son on your policy at least until he is 25, when his rates will be lower, or so I am told.

Another situation that is unique to a retired Boomer is

that wonderful time when your daughter becomes engaged. Of course, whether you are retired or not, the process is the same for every father—with one exception. When you are relatively young and retired from your job, you are perceived by family and friends as wealthy! This may or may not be true, but perception is stronger than reality. If you don't sponsor a lavish wedding, you are labeled a cheapskate.   I was prepared and looking forward to giving my daughter and her fiancé a beautiful wedding. I thought the best way to handle the financial side of the wedding was to give the "kids" a sum of money and then let them determine all the particulars, such as where to have the reception, how many people to invite, as well as the many decisions and details that are inherent in planning a wedding. I have always felt that I was a progressive dad, and this was their special time. Let them plan their wedding day so that they will be happy and comfortable with a minimum of parental involvement.

In theory this was a good strategy. As soon as my daughter was officially engaged, she initiated the blitzkrieg of potential sites for the wedding reception. She returned home from her maiden voyage armed with fancy brochures and colorful pictorials. To no one's surprise, I was hunkered down on the couch engrossed in watching a football game. Karin was all excited, "Dad we went to a lot of places, but there are two banquet facilities that are spectacular." She placed this huge mound of paper on the couch and left to make a phone call. I picked up her two favorite brochures, all the time keeping one eye glued to the television. At the next time out I studied the two marketing advertisements. I was in awe. How did they manage to transport Buckingham Palace and the Gardens of Versailles to New Jersey? I quickly thumbed through the two pamphlets looking for the cost per person of the reception. Talk about sticker shock. I thought I had put aside a significant amount of money for the wedding, but based on these two places, I only had enough for the down payment! I was in a quandary. I wanted Karin and Tito to be happy with their choice for a wedding reception, but I didn't want to spend the rest of my retirement traveling the New York City subways giving away pens in exchange for donations to the Dumb Dads in Debt Charity also known as Wedding Reception in 3D. If I abandoned the little common sense that I possessed, I would have the reception at one of these venues, but the guest list would have to be shredded to such an exclusive number that I might not invite myself. Fortunately, my daughter, seeing the perspiration dripping off my face, much like Ted Striker's sweaty brow when he tried to land the commercial jet in the movie *Airplane,* came to my rescue. "I know the cost is outrageous, Dad, but I just wanted you to see these fabulous estates that exist. I would much rather have a wedding at a more reasonable place and make sure that we invited all of our family and friends." I quickly responded before Karin had a change of heart, "If that is what you want, honey, then I am 100% supportive." Thanks to Karin, I avoided my first uncomfortable situation. Considering that the engagement was less than two days old, I was a little shaky on how this whole process would unfold.

Months have now passed, and I am happy to report that the wedding plans have gone about as smoothly as possible. However, I would be derelict in my duty, if I did not offer some sage advice to future fathers of the bride. How much input should a father contribute during the entire wedding process? Here is a clue. You should talk less than noted mime Marcel

Marceau. If you think that may be difficult, I suggest that you visit your local hardware store and purchase a roll of duct tape. Wrap your lips with the tape until you feel you could audition for a role in the movie *The Mummy,* thus giving you zero opportunity to verbalize a suggestion that you thought about sharing with your wife and daughter in a moment of weakness.

Men, don't look for support from your wife during the engagement cycle. Mother and daughter form a bond that is stronger than crazy glue. Your mission if you are willing to accept it is simple. Keep quiet, show up, and pay the bill. Fighting this directive is futile! Follow the words of the Rock, know your role! It's worked for me. I can't wait for Karin and Tito's wedding. If however, you have any advice on how to painlessly remove the duct tape, it would be greatly appreciated.

Additionally, by the time you have retired, you should have put into motion all the legal documents that will protect your spouse and your children. If you have not completed this assignment, you must contact an estate planning attorney ASAP!

The first building block to put your legal house in order is a simple letter of instruction. The form is not a legal document and certainly not a will, but it tells your family what to do and where your important papers are located in the event that you die. Eventually we all pass away, so this form will definitely be utilized. Mort and Alan Reisfield included this document in the seminar series entitled Financial Strategies for Successful Retirement, which I attended a number of years ago. Take the time to fill out this form! You will be doing the right thing for your family by giving them some direction at a very stressful time.

HAS ANYONE SEEN MY READING GLASSES?

A. FIRST THINGS TO DO

(1) Call _____ to help. (2) Notify employer _____
(relative or friend)   (phone)

(3) Make arrangements with funeral home.

(4) Request at least 10 copies of the death certificate (usually the funeral director will get them).

(5) Call lawyer _____ (6) Contact local Social Security office.
(name & phone)

(6) Get and process insurance policies. (7) Notify bank that holds our home mortgage.

B. LOCATION OF PERSONAL PAPERS

Last will and testament: _____   Birth Certificate: _____

Marriage Certificate: _____   Military Records: _____

Naturalization Papers: _____   Other (adoption) _____

C. SAVINGS ACCOUNTS AND CERTIFICATES *

Bank: _____ Address _____
Names on account _____
Type of Account _____ Account number _____
Location of passbook _____

Bank: _____ Address _____
Names on account _____
Type of Account _____ Account number _____
Location of passbook _____

Bank: _____ Address _____
Names on account _____
Type of Account _____ Account number _____
Location of passbook _____

* The bank must by law freeze the owner's accounts as soon as notified at death, even if jointly owned.

D. CHECKING ACCOUNTS *

Bank: _____ Address _____
Names on account _____
Type of Account _____ Account number _____
Location of passbook _____

Repeat to cover all accounts of husband and wife; canceled checks and statements are in:

_____

* The bank must by law freeze the owner's accounts as soon as notified at death, even if jointly owned.

E. INVESTMENT ACCOUNTS

Financial institution _____ Address _____
Names on account _____ Account number _____
Financial Advisor: _____ Telephone number _____
Location of statements _____

Financial institution _____ Address _____
Names on account _____ Account number _____
Financial Advisor: _____ Telephone number _____
Location of statements _____

F. SOCIAL SECURITY

Name _____ Card number _____
Location of card _____

File claim immediately to avoid possibility of losing any benefit checks. Call local office for appointment. They will tell you what to bring.
Phone _____

G. SAFE DEPOSIT BOX *

Bank _____ Address _____
In whose name _____ Number _____ Location of key _____
List of contents _____
_____
_____
_____

* In the event of death, the bank must by law seal the owner's box as soon as notified, even if jointly owned.

H. MONEY YOU CAN EXPECT

From my employer _____
                                    (person to contact phone)
_____
(life insurance)   (profit sharing)

From Insurance Companies: _____
From Social Security: _____ From other Souces: _____

I. LIFE INSURANCE

Location of all policies _____
Policy: _____ Insurance Co.: _____
        (Amount)
Company Address: _____
Kind of Policy: _____ Policy #: _____
Beneficiaries: _____
Issue Date: _____ Payout Options: _____
Other special facts: _____
Repeat information above for each policy

J. OTHER INSURANCE

Accident
Company: _____   Address: _____

Policy No: _____   Beneficiary: _____
Coverage: _____   Location of Policy: _____
Agent, if any: _____

Car, Home and Household
Give information below for each policy.

Coverage: _____   Company: _____
Address: _____
Policy No.: _____   Location of Policy: _____
Term (when to renew): _____   Agent, if any: _____

Medical Coverage
Company: _____   Address: _____
Policy No.: _____   Location of Policy: _____
Through employer or other group: _____   Agent, if any: _____
Repeat for all of the insurance policies.

Mortgage Insurance
Company: _____   Policy No: _____
Location of policy: _____

K. CAR

Year, make and model: _____
License No.: _____   Identification No.: _____
Location of papers: _____
(title, registration)

L. Credit Cards

All credit cards in my name should be canceled or converted to your name.
Company: _____   Phone: _____   Address: _____
Name on Card: _____   Number: _____
Location of Card _____
Repeat for each card

M. Investments

Stocks
Company: _____   Name on Certif.: _____   Number of Shares _____
Certificate no(s): _____   Purchase price and date: _____
Location of certif.: _____
Bonds / Notes / Bills
Issuer: _____   Issued to: _____
Face amount: _____   Bond No.: _____
Purchase price and date: _____   Maturity date: _____
Location of Certif. _____
Mutual Funds
Company: _____   Name of Fund _____
Name on account: _____   No. of Shares: _____
Location of statements, certificates: _____
Other investments (US Savings Bonds, etc.)
Repeat for each investment

N. Income Tax Returns

Location of all previous returns - federal, state, local:
_____   Our tax preparer: _____

O. House, Condo or Co-op

In whose name: _____ Address: _____
Lot: _____ Block: _____
Our lawyer at closing: _____
Location of statement of closing, policy or title ins., deed, land survey, etc.: _____

Mortgage held by: _____ Amount of orig. mortgage _____
Date taken out: _____ Amount owed now: _____
Method of payment: _____ Life ins. on mortgage? _____
Other important information: _____

P. Doctors' Names / Addresses

Doctors: _____
Dentists: _____
Pediatrician: _____
Others: _____

Q. Relatives, Friends to Inform

List names, addresses, phone numbers
_____
_____
_____
_____

R. Cemetery and Funeral

Cemetery Plot
Location: _____ When purchased: _____
Deed no.: _____ Location of Deed _____
Other information _____

Facts for Funeral Director (bring this with you, and bring cemetery deed if possible)
My Full Name _____ Residence _____
Phone: _____ Marital Status: _____ Spouse _____
Birth Date: _____ Birthplace: _____
Father's name and birthplace: _____
Mother's maiden name _____
Military Service: _____ When: _____ Social Security Number: _____
Occupation: _____

When your letter is done...

1. Keep revising it. As time goes by, your personal matters may change.

2. You will want to update your letter at least once every year, for instance, at tax time. Or, depending on your personal situation, you might want to update it even more often.

3. Send the revisions to the same people to whom you sent the original.

4. Clip a copy to your wills and keep a copy in a place your family would turn to first.

I am not an attorney, and would not profess to give legal advice to anyone, but all retired Boomers should have at a minimum executed the following documents:

1.   The Last Will and Testament
2.   Power of Attorney
3.   Advanced Directive for Health Care

The following is a brief overview of these legal documents:

The Last Will and Testament allows you to exercise control over how your assets are to be distributed, and appoint the person you want to handle your affairs after your death.

Power of Attorney is an instrument in writing by which you appoint another as your agent, and give him the authority to perform certain specified acts on your behalf. The authority of the Power of Attorney terminates upon your death.

Advanced Directive for Health Care is a document that gives instructions about your health care, if in the future you can not speak for yourself. The document allows you to name an agent whom you empower to make health care decisions for you. You may also give instructions about the kind of health care you do or do not want.

As we grow older and our children mature into adulthood, it is quite likely that you will appoint one of your children to be the executor of your will. This is an awesome responsibility for your child. It is incumbent on us to communicate to our children our wishes and desires, and make sure that these are reflected in the proper legal documents.

Now that you have put your legal affairs in order, you have accomplished several goals. For some, you have made life easier for your family in what should be a very emotional and stressful time. For others, you have prevented your children from declaring you mentally incompetent because you misplaced your reading glasses.

We are parents, but we are also children. If your mom and dad are still alive you are very fortunate. If your parents died before their time, I'm sure you carry an empty feeling that probably never goes away. As retired Boomers we have the opportunity to spend more time with our parents, but the uncertainty and concern for their future is a dark cloud that impacts upon our retirement decisions. There is a litany of questions that we silently ask ourselves over and over again. How is my parents' health? What would I do if they became ill? If I move away to a retirement community, will I be abandoning my parents at a time when they need me the most? What is their financial situation? What are their wishes and instructions as they get older? Do they have wills? What type of elder care is in their best interest?

Until I retired, most of these questions were more like faint whispers in my head. For the most part, my parents were in good health, and I was focused on making a living and concentrating my efforts on my immediate family. When I retired, and became a little less self absorbed, I approached my dad to get answers to my questions. Now, understand my father is an intelligent man. I asked him a simple question. "Do you have a will?" His response stunned me. "A will—why do I need a will? Once I am dead, I'm dead". In an instant I realized that I was guilty for not broaching the subject a long time ago. I explained to him why it was not only vital for him to have the necessary legal documents, but without clear instructions, he was potentially going to make my life miserable as the person who would be responsible for his affairs. Once he understood the concept and the ramifications of his actions, he was eager to implement my suggestions.

This experience taught me a valuable lesson. You should not assume your parents are savvy in the ways of the world (amazingly, my children realized this fact about their father at a very tender age), and you must confront the issue of your parents' mortality even if it is a topic that both parent and child are reluctant to engage in.

Sadly, my wife lost both her parents within a two year span during my retirement. As the son-in-law you walk a fine line when your spouse's mom and dad's health decline. You want to be supportive and helpful, but in the final analysis it is the children who will be responsible for making very difficult decisions affecting their parents.

My father-in-law was a wonderful man. He was the picture of health until the last year of his life. He never went to a doctor, took no medication, and was mentally sharp. At the age of eighty-eight he and his wife were living independently in their own home performing all the usual duties and activities consistent with any independent elderly couple. His only concession to age was that he reluctantly agreed to hand over the car keys. Bill took full responsibility for caretaking my mother-in-law whose physical and mental capacities were beginning to decline. It was generally assumed by the family that my mother-in-law would be the first to leave us, and if it were possible, Bill would live forever.

To everyone's surprise, it was Bill whose health rapidly deteriorated. My wife, my brother-in-law, Ken, and I had absolutely no experience on how to confront this problem. I suspect that many Boomers are in or will be in a similar situation. I hope for your sake that you will be better prepared to handle this eventuality. Our problems were compounded when I found out that Bill and his children had literally no discussion concerning all the legal documents that have been discussed in the beginning of this chapter. We did not know if certain legal documents existed. Bill had never sat his children down to outline his instructions in preparation for his death, and the children were more than happy not to engage him in this vital but morbid subject.

As Bill's health declined, decisions had to be made on what would be the best health care alternative. He was incapable of taking care of himself and he was the main care giver for his wife. After considering the various options, the family decided to bring a licensed health care provider to live in the house for twenty-four hours a day during the week. Ken and my wife would take turns living at my in-laws' house on the weekends.

The idea of bringing someone to live in your parent's house is a scary proposition. We had heard all the horror stories of supposed care givers mistreating and pilfering from the elderly that they were hired to protect, but we really did not have much of a choice. Even in Bill's physically and mentally diminished state, he was not going to leave his home voluntarily and enter a health care facility. Initially, neither Ken nor my wife had power of attorney, so making difficult decisions that were in the best interest of their father was sometimes a mute point. We contacted a local health care staffing provider, did due diligence, checked references, and interviewed the woman who would be responsible for the heath and welfare of my in-laws. Even after we concluded that this licensed care giver was a perfect fit to watch over Bill, we closed our eyes and crossed our fingers, hoping that we had made the wise choice for our parents.

When this type of situation is thrust upon you and you have not done the proper planning, you find yourself in a mad scramble to make sure that you do the right thing. You have plenty of questions but few answers. Why didn't I see the signs that my father's health was failing? Could I have done something differently to help him? Am I being selfish for not caring for my parents in my own home? What if my father gets worse? What do I do next? How do I protect my father's assets? How do we pay for this home care? Where are my dad's important documents, bills, insurance policies, etc.? If my father dies, what is the best course of action for my mother? If you are the type of person who is susceptible to pangs of quilt, real or imagined, you are in store for many sleepless nights. Unfortunately, in spite of all the well-meaning advice, the only cure is time.

The woman we hired to tend to Bill and his wife proved to be a God-send. Thalia was a Jamaican-born immigrant who appreciated her adopted country more than most native born Americans. She possessed the patience of Job and watched over Bill to the very end. When he passed away, it was in his own house in his own bedroom. Knowing Bill, that's the way he would have wanted it.

I can't say enough nice things about Thalia, the nurse, and the people from hospice. They made the last months of Bill's life as comfortable as possible. Their passion for their work and their compassion for the sick were remarkable.

Once Bill had passed away, we had to make decisions concerning my mother-in-law's care. Her physical and mental condition differed from her husband's. Although she was weak, she was not physically ill. However, she was suffering from dementia and was in the early stages of Alzheimer's disease. We ruled out the possibility of home care. Having live-in assistance would have been equivalent to hiring a forty thousand dollar a year babysitter. Plus by this time, spending every weekend at your parents' home was becoming an arduous experience for

Ken and Ethel. After talking to doctors, the family made the decision to move Mom into a health care facility. Thalia would continue to live at the house and oversee Mom's needs until we found the right place that best matched her physical and mental condition.

Once again, like so many Boomers who are put in this position, we were treading on unexplored territory. There is an enormous amount of health care options available today, from senior housing with medical assistance, to nursing homes that look and feel like a miniature hospital. My mother-in-law was past the point of living an independent existence but was not in the family's opinion, nursing home material. Depending on the level of care, each facility has its own price tag, and just like any other competitive business, the cost varies even among facilities that cater to people with similar needs. Based on my mother-in-law's health, I estimated correctly that the cost for her care would be about forty thousand dollars per year.

We started to interview various health care providers. Some disqualified my mother-in-law because her needs were beyond their capacity. Others did not give us a good level of comfort that Mom would be cared for properly. I turned to the computer and went on the internet. I found a referral service that gave me an education about the health care process. I filled out an online form that asked detailed questions about my mother-in-law's status, and what the family was looking to accomplish. The service came back with four places that they recommended. They followed up my internet session with a phone call that proved to be very informative. Based on our conversation and the data that I had submitted, they recommended Potomac Homes.

We visited Potomac, and immediately had a good feeling about the place. The house was in a residential area surrounded by a white picket fence. It looked very similar to the other well-groomed homes in the neighborhood. The facility specialized in servicing people with dementia and Alzheimer's. The sense was that you were in your own home, albeit one with a number of overnight quests. Most importantly, we were impressed with the attitude and disposition of the staff. As a bonus, the home was opening a new facility that would be five minutes from where my wife and I live.

Once we had secured the new living environment for Mom, we had to start the process of selling her house to pay the expenses for her new home. Selling the house, like so many aspects of eldercare, can become a very prickly matter between the children. Parting with the house that you grew up with and where your parents have lived their whole lives is an emotional as well as economic decision. Many relationships between siblings have been severed during the eldercare process, and when decisions have financial implications that unfortunately bring out the worst in people. Thankfully, Ken and Ethel have a strong bond and all decisions were made with only one thought in mind. What is in the best interests of our parent? The house was eventually sold. Like any real estate transaction, there was plenty of aggravation before the process was completed.

Life in a home filled with people with Alzheimer's is at the same time both rewarding and disturbing. You feel good that your loved one is living in a beautiful house
, getting quality care, and is interacting with both staff and other patients. Yet, seeing people, especially those who are in the elevated stages of Alzheimer's, walking around with blank expressions on their faces, is by any standard depressing.

On one of my first trips to visit my mother-in-law, I was greeted by a woman whom I guessed to be in her late seventies.

She was very well dressed, and looked as if she were going out to a fancy social function. In a German accent, she said, "You're a handsome young man. Do you want to hear a story about my childhood?" I thought to myself, this lady is too sharp to be a patient here, and if she is, then at least she possesses wonderful eyesight. "Sure" I responded.

We sat down on the couch and for the next fifteen minutes she described in detail her life in Germany as a young child. She mentioned specific dates and referenced places in great detail. I was amazed at the memory that this lady possessed. She spoke to me as if these events occurred yesterday, not sixty or seventy years ago. I needed to use the men's room and excused myself. I remember thinking, "Why is this woman here?" I can't remember what I ate for breakfast, and I usually misplace my reading glasses two or three times a day; meanwhile this lady has just recited her personal diary dating back prior to World War Two.

I returned to the sitting area to continue our conversation. My new friend approached me. I smiled at her and she said, "You're a handsome young man. Do you want to hear a story about my childhood?" I wasn't sure if the lady was putting me on, or if I had discovered why she was living at the home. Sadly, quickly, it became obvious that the latter was true. She had no idea who I was or that we had this conversation five minutes earlier. I said, "Sure," and proceeded to hear an encore presentation of her youth. I'm ashamed to say this, but since I knew the tale that she was about to tell me, I couldn't resist razzling and dazzling her with my own intimate knowledge of Germany in the nineteen thirties. It was fresh in my mind because I had only learned about it five minutes earlier. I described in detail how beautiful the countryside was, especially in the spring when the flowers would bloom.

She was wide eyed. She had found a kindred spirit who shared her experiences. Utilizing my uncanny ability for matching accents with birth places, coupled with the fact that this woman had just told me her life story, I was able to pinpoint exactly in Germany where she was born and raised. She was flabbergasted, and I was thinking of changing my name to The Amazing Kreskin. Eventually, I left Potomac and headed for home. I wondered if I really had given this woman some solace during my visit. Probably not! But the experience did give me a powerful insight into the life of an Alzheimer's patient.

My mother-in-law stayed at Potomac Home for a year and a half and passed away peacefully without having to be moved to a more intensive health care facility. We were very fortunate that both of my wife's parents passed away without incurring long painful illnesses. The families that have to deal with that issue deserve all the empathy and support we can muster. The eldercare experiences that my family lived through taught us a lot about the process. The following are some additional pieces of advice that may be of use to you when you face the inevitable task of caring for your parents.

The first thing that you want to do when your parents start getting on in age is to locate a good eldercare attorney. From my experience and the experiences of others, two common mistakes occur: Hiring an attorney at the last minute, and utilizing a generalist instead of a specialist. The person who represented you when you closed on your house or defended you against a speeding violation is usually not the most competent individual to handle the eldercare process. Start engaging in the legal documentation when your parents are healthy, both physically and mentally. You have a much better chance to protect their assets and comply with their wishes. A typical scenario for many Boomers is to do no financial and legal planning for their parents until a grave illness occurs. A mad scramble ensues as the children try to shift assets from their parent's estate to themselves to avoid the hospital and nursery home costs that threaten to empty their life savings. Unfortunately Uncle Sam is wise to this gambit and you must show a clear paper trail that demonstrates that your parents have no income or liquid assets for a minimum of three years. A good eldercare attorney is worth the price to navigate you through these types of complex situations.

Don't be divorced from your parents' financial circumstances. Older people are prime targets for both unscrupulous con men as well as legitimate companies who view seniors as an easy mark to peddle financial products that are not in the best interests of their clients. Case in point, my father-in-law was persuaded to convert his money market account with a local bank to a variable annuity, through their newly opened affiliated brokerage group. The bank demonstrated wonderful customer service to Bill. He was eighty-six years old when they made their sales pitch. The bank offered to do the closing at Bill's home where he could sign all the financial documents. The annuity made no financial sense for a man of his age. When Bill passed away, the bank made it as difficult as possible for his contract to be liquidated and the money transferred to my mother-in-law. They cited withdrawal penalty clauses which if activated would reduce the value of the contract significantly. The money was now tied up and could not be utilized to pay for the care of my mother-in-law, a circumstance that Bill would not have wanted for his wife. The amount of time and aggravation that my wife had to invest to rectify this blatant corporate opportunism was sinful.

I mentioned this earlier but it bears repeating: educate yourself on the eldercare process. The internet offers advice, support groups, and directories of all types of companies and organizations that are part of the process. Many of these groups offer assistance to you with no fee or cost.

It is imperative that someone in the family has the power of attorney for an ailing loved one. My wife had that responsibility for her parents. However, we did not anticipate that every financial outfit involved in the process wanted their own power of attorney form to be signed in addition to the one we had already executed. Even Medicare requested that a new form be filled out. When your loved one is no longer mentally competent, that is the time when you are going to take over making decisions for them. It doesn't make sense to me that you must thrust a pen in front of someone who may not be physically or mentally capable of making an informed decision. Isn't that why you did due diligence and executed the power of attorney in the first place? Also, be advised your power of attorney will be useless if your parents have assets (bank accounts, real-estate) in other states different from the state where the power of attorney was drawn up. As an example, if your parents granted you power of attorney when they lived in New Jersey and eventually they move to a different state, you will not be able to make decisions on the assets located in the new state. You must have a new power of attorney drawn up.

Further, I think it is wise to prepay and plan the funeral in advance of the love one's passing. You have complied with their wishes and the expense of the funeral will be paid out of the deceased's estate. Most importantly, it is one less thing to have to worry about during a painful and stressful time.

Lastly, utilize your experience to benefit others who are going through the eldercare process. You will be providing them with valuable knowledge and in return telling your story to others will make your loss a little easier to bear.

CHAPTER 11
Long term care Insurance

In general, as you approach retirement you should carefully review all your insurance policies. You may be surprised when you add up all the premiums that you are paying for, including life, health, auto, homeowner, and various other insurances. If you are like me, you probably know that you should periodically audit these policies, but unless you experience a major life change such as retirement, inheritance, or job loss, who really bothers?

Here are a few examples. You were employed by a major corporation. Your wife stayed home to raise the children. You had a huge life insurance policy to protect your family and pay off the mortgage if you were to die prematurely. Well, your kids are grown up. The mortgage is paid off, and you are no longer employed. Review the policy! Is it term or whole life? If it is term, when will the term end and how much will your rates increase if you renew the insurance? What will it cost you today to lock into less coverage? I mentioned earlier the cost and aggravation that you incur when you leave your children on your automobile insurance policy. But how many people are paying collision insurance for an older car? The premium could be more than the value of the car! If your health care is not subsidized in your retirement or, in other words, you are not a former teacher, policeman, or government employee, you have inherited a major cost to your budget. Should you purchase catastrophic insurance and pay most of your health bills out of your pocket, take a traditional health plan with a high deductible, or become part of an HMO? That being said, I want to explore a type of insurance that has become very popular with the Baby Boomers—long term health care. The marketing of this product is geared almost exclusively to Baby Boomers. The Generation X group is too young to worry about their old age and the Greatest Generation has lost their window of opportunity if they did not subscribe when these policies first emerged. As the premiums for these polices are age-based, the cost for older Americans is astronomical. I chronicled in the previous chapter my experiences with the long term care process for my in-laws. The focus in this chapter is to give you a clearer picture of the benefits, pitfalls, and costs of this insurance product and to help determine if this coverage is right for you.

The following are some facts and statistics concerning long term health care:

- Every seven seconds a person turns fifty in the United States.
- Approximately one in every four households is involved in caring for the needs of someone older than fifty.
- Americans spend eighty three billion dollars annually on nursing home care.
- By the year 2031, every Baby Boomer will be over sixty-five years old.
- The average cost for one year in an assisted living facility is over thirty thousand dollars.
- One year in a private room at a nursing home will cost over seventy thousand dollars.

- The number of Americans who have purchased long term care has more than tripled over the last decade.
- A home health care aid will cost you about eighteen dollars an hour.
- Medical insurance and Medicare will for all practical purposes not cover your long term care expenses.
- Nearly five million Americans are currently afflicted with Alzheimer's.

Long term insurance covers an insured when the individual needs assistance in the activities of daily living, which include basic activities such as eating, dressing, bathing, toileting, transferring, (moving in or out of a bed, chair, or wheelchair), and continence.

Most long term care policies will cover the cost of nursing homes, assisted living facilities, and in-home care. The insured must be able to demonstrate that he can no longer perform at least two activities of daily living for a period of at least ninety days. The majority of insurance policies include Alzheimer's disease and advance dementia as conditions that qualify to receive benefits.

The biggest motivation to purchase a long term care policy is to preserve the assets and savings that you have accumulated during your life. The fear that an illness in your later years will leave you financially and medically dependent on your children's assistance is, for some, a sobering thought. Plus, not being able to leave your children an inheritance is disconcerting.

People with assets of less than two hundred thousand dollars are not candidates for this type of insurance. The premiums would eat up too much of their holdings. If you are very wealthy and money is not an object, you might want to self-insure yourself and put money aside for a potential catastrophic illness. That leaves people who have assets ranging from more than two hundred thousand dollars to about two million dollars. This large group is the prime demographic for long term care insurance.

If you fall into this category does that mean that you should purchase long term insurance? Not necessarily. Your decision will be based on many factors, such as the cost of the plan, your health, and family medical history. If you believe that you will not receive the benefits of the policy, will you be motivated to make the premiums?

Once you have decided to examine competing long term care policies, you will be as mystified as you were when you tried to solve the Rubik's Cube puzzle. These policies offer a myriad of options and choices. It is often difficult to compare policies from different companies. One company may offer a benefit that is important to you and while you think another carrier also gives you the same benefit, the verbiage in the contract is not exactly the same and must be interpreted carefully.

Of course, a key question to be answered when doing your due diligence on long term insurance is what the policy is going to cost. If you are like me, you may have no clue as to how much the premiums will cost you. For illustration purposes, the following is a rate quote that I received from AARP Health Care Options, which is underwritten by Metropolitan Life Insurance Company. This personalized rate quote was written in February of 2005, just prior to my fifty-fifth birthday. The rate was based on the then current age of fifty-four. The company offered three prepackaged plans: basic, choice and select. I found this option to be very helpful in making an informed decision by comparing the benefits vs. the cost of the premiums.

Personalized Rate Quote for your current age of 54.

	Basic Plan	Choice Plan	Select Plan
Total Benefit Amount **Monthly Benefit Amount (MBA)** 100% for care in an assisted living facility or nursing home	$87,600 $1,800 a month (4 years of care*)	$175,200 $3,600 a month (4 years of care*)	No Dollar Limit $3,600 a month (coverage for as long as you need care)
Monthly Benefit Amount 50% for care at home or an adult day care center	(Not Included)	$1,800	$1,800
Monthly Premium with Future Purchase Increase	$26.70	$65.16	$102.84
Monthly Premium with Future Purchase Increase and 30% Household Discount	$18.69	$45.61	$71.99
Monthly Premium with Automatic Inflation Protection	$68.04	$159.48	$271.92
Monthly Premium with Automatic Inflation Protection and 30% Household Discount	$47.63	$111.64	$190.34
"Informal care" (up to 50% of the monthly home care benefit)	(Not included)	✓	✓
Waiver of Premium (premiums are waived when you begin receiving payment of benefits for certain covered services.)	✓	✓	✓
Deductible Period: 30 days, **once in your lifetime**	✓	✓	✓
Restoration of Benefits	✓	✓	✓

*May be longer if you don't use the full benefit amount each month.
When two AARP members in the same household apply and are accepted for coverage, each is eligible for a 30% Household Discount.
Basic Plan not available in Vermont.
Note: A variety of options are also available at an additional cost. Please see the application or speak to one of our long-term care insurance consultants for details. Coverage under this plan is intended to be tax qualified. Consult your tax advisor for details.

The purchase of a long term care policy carries a double-edged sword for the insured. On one hand, once you have purchased the policy, your rates cannot be raised. However, your premiums can be increased for entire groups of policy holders. Many insurance companies underpriced their policies in the nineteen eighties and nineties. They did not foresee the rising cost of health care. These firms have the ability to ask state insurance commissions for premium increases. This unpublished loophole has in fact been utilized by a majority of companies, and rates have increased. If you are an older policy holder and your rates increase, your options are not pretty. If you can not afford the increase, you run the risk of turning in your policy, having no insurance, and flushing the years of paid premiums down the toilet. When considering a policy, it is wise to find out the insurance company's history in asking and being granted increases in premiums.

The entire concept of long term health care makes perfect sense to me, but the ability of the insurance companies to raise premiums has given me cause for concern. As of today, I have not inked my name on a long term policy. I do, however, have several friends who have purchased long term care policies.

Dennis and Denise Textor and Ken and Linda Ballan have some unique experiences with the subject. The following are highlights from interviews that I conducted with them.

Dennis purchased long term policies for both him and his wife in nineteen ninety nine, just prior to his fiftieth birthday. He did a lot of comparison shopping, checking out all the major insurance firms that offered long term care policies. To his surprise the policy that worked best for him and was the most economical was written by Thrivent Financial for Lutherans. Thrivent, according to their web site, is a faith-based membership organization. It is a fraternal benefit society able to sell insurance products and required by law to be non-profit. They conduct charitable benevolent social and educational programs and activities to benefit their members and the community in which they live. Thrivent has nearly three million members and has assets under management of sixty—three billon dollars.

The cost and benefits of the insurance, the low overhead, tax exempt non-profit status and the strong relationship with his faith made the choice an easy one for Dennis. This proved to be very beneficial to the Textor's. Thrivent, like many other financial firms, underestimated the escalating health care costs. Rather than seeking a premium increase from the various state insurance commissioners, Thrivent simply decided not to sell any additional policies. They now act as an agent for a large insurance carrier for new long term care policies and focus their attention on the financial service products that they underwrite directly. What this means for Dennis is that he is locked into a great deal. Similar to the old Hebrew National commercial, they are responsible to a higher authority! Dennis maintains that once he is certified to receive his monthly benefit, meaning, he is in an assisted living or nursing home, Thrivent will pay him fully his contracted benefit even if the monthly cost of his stay is less than the contracted benefit. He is confident that because of the unique structure of the contract, he will not be subjected to supplying excessive monthly paperwork required by many insurance carriers. In other words, once he is admitted to a care facility and deemed by the insurance company to be eligible for benefits, he will receive his monthly benefit check automatically. Based on my interview with Dennis, I am strongly considering becoming a Lutheran. I hope church officials will agree with me that the ability to purchase a quality long term care policy is a sincere motivation to become one of the flock.

Ken and Linda Ballan are not only long term care insurance policy holders, but their parents purchased policies when the product was still in its infancy. Ken's mother purchased a long term care policy in the mid-nineties. The contract at that time only covered in-home care. It did not cover nursing homes and assisted living facilities. Ken's mom paid the premiums for the policy for about five years. When her doctor verified that she was in the first stages of Alzheimer's, she was able to recover one hundred and ten dollars a day, (the amount of the contract) for two years to offset the expense of having twenty-four hour in-home care. Prior to his mother getting a long term care policy, Ken really did not have a very good handle on what long term care insurance was all about. Initially when the product became available, the people who were investigating purchasing the insurance were generally elderly. That contrasts with today's policy holders whose average age is sixty-two. Since the cost of the premiums is aged-based, a strong case can be made for purchasing sooner vs. later.

Linda's father purchased a policy when his wife contracted cancer. He wanted to make sure that if he were forced to go to a health care facility he wouldn't squander his remaining assets. The policy has proven to be successful as the cost of his care has exceeded the premiums he has paid. The one area that has been a significant headache for Linda was the submission of paperwork when her father was admitted to a health care facility. The root of her problem was that as her father's illness worsened, he was moved and received treatment from doctors in New York, New Jersey, and Florida. The insurance company required doctor certification on a daily basis to pay out the benefit claim. It was a logistical nightmare to get multiple doctors in different locations to sign off. It took Linda six months to get the process on track. Linda is a business manager for State Health Policy which is part of Rutgers University. She admitted she needed help from other industry professionals to solve the problem. According to Linda, without a health care advocate, an insured would find the certification process impossible. The good news for Linda is now that the initial verification process has been validated, the benefits are being paid on a regular basis.

About six years ago Ken and Linda looked into the possibility of a long term care policy for themselves. At the time Linda was not convinced that they needed this insurance. Fortunately, Ken's mom was still in good health and was not receiving benefits yet, so their knowledge was somewhat limited. One insurance agent gave Ken the best answer to his question, "Why do we need the coverage"? His reply was,"Because you can get it." He explained to Ken that presently both he and Linda were both healthy which made this the perfect time to get the coverage. Should either one of them become ill in the future, the chances of becoming insured with a long term care policy would be in jeopardy or at the very least, the premiums would skyrocket. I think many people associate long term care with elderly people who have contracted Alzheimer's and who reside in nursing homes. There are however, many younger people who are confined to a health care facility who because of cancer, heart attack, stroke and a variety of illnesses, cannot perform at least two activities of daily living. This point became crystal clear to Ken when two years ago he suffered a heart attack.

After shopping different companies, Ken and Linda purchased a policy from CNA Insurance. One benefit that was very appealing to them was a shared benefit option. Ken and Linda have their own individual policies. They also own a third policy. If one of them is receiving benefits and the benefits fall short of the health care expense, they can utilize this policy to make them whole. By purchasing multiple policies, they were able to get a discount on their premiums. They also opted for automatic inflation protection, where their benefits would increase five percent compounded to offset the rising cost of health care. Ken opted for a ninety day deductible period. He would rather be responsible for the first ninety days of care out of pocket and pay lower premiums for the duration of his policy.

Both the Textors and the Ballans are very happy that they made the investment into long term health care insurance. If they should need the benefit, it is there for them, and if they never recoup their premiums that's okay as well. Linda surprised me when she told me that many of her friends and co-workers in the late forties to sixty year old age group have recently signed on for long term care insurance. Further investigating revealed that many medium to large corporations are offering this insurance as part of their employee benefit program. How much if anything you save by utilizing this corporate benefit is subject to the individual firm's plan.

Two good sources of information to educate you on this subject are:

1. The Shoppers Guide to Long Term Care Insurance written by the National Association of Insurance Commissioners. They can be contacted by phone (816-842-3600) Fax (816-783-8175) and on the web www.naic.org

2. Long Term Care Planning Tool Kit created by the US Department of Health and Human Services. They can be contacted by phone (866-752-6582) The kit is being distributed by a five state pilot project team. The five states participating in the project are Arkansas, Idaho, Nevada, New Jersey and Virginia.

Now, I know what you are thinking. What ever became of Ken Ballan after he suffered his heart attack, and how come this chapter doesn't include a semi-entertaining story based on personal experience ostensibly to flow with the subject matter? Fortunately (for the purposes of this book), I was with Ken when he suffered his heart attack, proving once again that even under the direst circumstances a good story may surface.

Ken and I play golf together two or three times a year. We made arrangements to play at Flanders Valley Golf Course conveniently located five minutes from my house. The course is an excellent public facility owned and operated by Morris County. For me, if Flanders Valley were a bar it would be named Cheers like the famed television show, where everyone knows your name. In the spring and summer, the course is my home away from home. Over the years, I have gotten to know most of the people who work there. The staff is composed of retired individuals who work there to play golf for free and to socialize with the public in an office that consists of grass, sand, water, and thirty-six holes in the ground with sticks in them. The employees are fellow hackers who don't take themselves too seriously. This, in turn, provides for a golfer-friendly environment.

As I drove to the golf course to meet Ken, my thoughts were fixed on another matter. Several days earlier I had failed a stress test for the second time. I could not understand how someone as active as I with no family history of heart problems could be at risk. The insurance company who initiated the tests to renew my term life insurance must have been concerned because they denied me coverage. The only person not concerned was my cardiologist. He said I may have a problem, but we would need to take more sophisticated and reliable tests to determine if I indeed have something wrong with me. I am not a worrier, but my health status, coupled with the fact that if something happened to me, my wife and children would not have the benefit of an insurance policy, gave me an uncomfortable feeling.

Once I saw Ken at the golf course, my health concerns

disappeared. I had to focus on my golf checklist of things to do and not do during the two seconds it takes to swing a golf club. Fortunately for me my brain only has the capacity to worry about one thing at a time and playing golf would challenge my primitive level of concentration.

Ken was all pumped up to play golf. Unlike me, he was still working for a living, and taking a half day off to play golf on a beautiful sunny day was a treat. We got caught up with recent developments in our lives. We swapped stories about our children and exchanged information about the latest golf tips and equipment which would propel us from hacker status to the lofty perch of decent golfers. We decided to spice up our outing by playing a two dollar Nassau match. A Nassau bet is very common on the golf course. The golfer who wins the most holes in match play for the front nine holes wins the agreed upon wager. In this case, it would be two dollars. The same is true for the back nine holes and the golfer who wins the most total holes overall wins the agreed upon wager, which in our case would be an additional two dollars. The money isn't significant, but the bragging rights are.

Two older gentlemen in golf carts drove up to the tee box and introduced themselves. As has been my customary experience, these strangers proved to be good company. Our foursome teed off. They sped away in their cart and Ken and I grabbed our pull carts and lumbered down the fairway. The first three holes proceeded in an uneventful fashion. After Ken teed off on the fourth hole, he mentioned that he wasn't feeling quite right. He then walked up to his ball and hit one of the best shots that I had ever seen him execute.

I played my next shot and proceeded on my way. I looked for Ken and saw that he was bent over in obvious pain. I asked him where his pain was coming from and he said the upper abdomen. I asked him if he had any tightness in the chest or pain in his arm and he grunted no. I said to Ken, "I am sure it is nothing, but let's get you back to the clubhouse." Our problem was that we were deep into the golf course and we didn't have a golf cart to transport us back. Our playing partners, seeing Ken's condition and our plight, offered us their cart. We phoned the clubhouse via cell phone and they immediately called the rescue squad. I thanked the fellows for the loan of the cart and told them that I would be back ASAP. Up to this point, I thought Ken probably was hurting from acid indigestion, a gas pocket, or some other non-lifethreatening malady. I thought to myself, it is better to err on the side of caution, but on the other hand, why couldn't Ken get ill on the back nine or when I was playing poorly?

I glanced at Ken as I started the drive back to the clubhouse. His condition had worsened considerably. He was slumped in his seat with his eyes closed. Ken responded to my questions in a faint whisper. In an instant, reality hit me like a sledge hammer. My friend was having a heart attack.

I drove down the middle of the fairway making a beeline into the golfers who were hitting their tee shots. Initially they had no idea what was going on, and I found myself being attacked by golf balls. I felt like a tank commander plowing forward while the enemy is firing missiles. Kenny is now barely conscious. I have to hold him with my right hand so that he does not fall out of the cart. I am driving the cart like a lunatic with my left hand and screaming at the top of my lungs, "Medical emergency, get out of my way." Of course, on the golf course nobody can really hear you until you get into close proximity. The groups of golfers that I have invaded probably think that Ken and I are either drunk or crazy. A ranger tries to cut me off and screams out to me. "What the hell are you doing?" I am a crazed animal. I tell him to go &%*# himself.

I make it to the clubhouse and the police and Flanders Rescue Squad are waiting. They quickly and efficiently tend to Ken and tell Ken and me that the paramedics are on their way. They pull me off to the side and tell me that everything is going to be all right and that Ken will be taken to Morristown Memorial Hospital. I want to be with my friend but I remember that I have the golf cart and the golf clubs of our playing partners. I need someone to follow me out to the fairway and then bring me back to the clubhouse so I can go to the hospital. There is no one in the clubhouse that can taxi me back. So, I sprint from the clubhouse to the cart shed and explain my predicament to the person in charge. The car supervisor says he is the only person on duty and he can't leave his post. As my eyes start to bulge and my voice gets louder, he reconsiders. I run back to the clubhouse, hop on the cart and race back to the spot where Ken became ill, with the cart supervisor following closely.

Once again I am screaming and waving my arms as I interrupt groups of golfers. I arrive back at the spot where my two golfing companions are waiting. I thank them profusely for lending me their cart and confide in them that they may have saved a life. I quickly take Ken's and my clubs and load them on the supervisor's cart. The golf course is now totally backed up with three groups of golfers mulling around the same spot. No one is quite sure what the proper protocol is in a situation like this. I jump in the supervisors cart and start to leave, when one of my former playing partners shouts out, "Pat, we have a problem!" These are not our golf clubs.

At first I had no explanation, but then I realized what happened. When I ran back to the clubhouse, in my haste, and not being able to recognize my playing partners' golf clubs, I jumped into the wrong golf cart! I'm really in a bad way now. Fortunately, the cart supervisor steps up and tells the club less golfers he will straighten everything out and return their clubs as soon as he transports me back to the ambulance.

On the ride back, I took mental inventory of what had just occurred. My friend had a heart attack. I had succeeded in creating chaos in the middle of the golf course. I had misplaced the golf cart and clubs from the playing partners who lent them to me. I verbally assaulted an elderly ranger. I now have the equipment of two unsuspecting strangers who probably think that their golf clubs have been stolen and are filing a police report. To my way of thinking, only Frankenstein and the Blues Brothers had more people after them than I, and I accomplished this in less than thirty minutes.

I arrived back at the clubhouse just as the ambulance was leaving for the hospital. Even with an oxygen tank by his side and two IV's hanging from his arms, Ken looked much better than he did earlier. As the ambulance doors are closing, Ken whips off the oxygen mask like a catcher spotting a foul pop up and says, "Grab my wallet, and bring my insurance card. Call my wife and drive my car to the hospital." The paramedic slaps the mask back on him and off they go to the hospital with sirens blaring. I'm impressed with Kenny's attention for detail especially considering the circumstances. I guess the public perception of CPA's is all wrong. Sure, they live a rock star-like existence, partying to the wee hours of the morning, and hanging out with the rich and famous, yet if Ken is representative of this group, they must be tough hombres.

I rummage through Ken's golf bag and quickly find his wallet. Unfortunately, after ten minutes I still cannot find his keys. Finally, I empty out the entire contents on the pavement and spy the keys camouflaged between golf gloves and a divot repair tool.

I'm in panic mode now. I have to get to the hospital to fulfill Kenny's requests and I am behind schedule. I hoist the two golf bags over my shoulders and shuffle into the parking lot. I grab Ken's car keys and realize that I don't have the faintest idea which car is Ken's. The keys are attached to a remote door opener. I throw the golf clubs on the ground and proceed to walk up and down the rows of cars clicking away like a madman, hoping that a car trunk is going to fly open. Two thirds of the way into my pilgrimage a trunk pops open. I am still wary. What if this somehow is not Ken's car? Then I can add grand theft auto to my escalating rap sheet. I check his glove compartment for identification and start the ignition with his key. Satisfied, I head for the hospital.

On the way to the hospital I have the unenviable task of calling Linda and telling her that Ken has had a heart attack. I give her all the particulars and continue with my mission. All sorts of thoughts are swirling in my head. My friend has just suffered a heart attack which arrived without warning or invitation, yet I am the one who has failed two stress tests. I'm probably more at risk than he was! Is Ken going to be okay or will he be limited to a restricted life style? Should I always utilize a golf cart in the future? If we didn't have the use of the golf cart, what would have happened to Ken? After my keystone cop-like rescue mission, did all the golfers get their own golf clubs returned to them?

I arrived at the hospital and headed for the admissions desk. Once I completed the paper work, they allowed me to visit Ken. He was alert and just like the scene in the ambulance he was being fed oxygen and morphine. I didn't know the full extent of Ken's health, so I tackled the situation with my best weapon, my sense of humor. I told him that his playacting on the golf course was a bit excessive just to avoid paying a few dollars for a losing golf bet. I conveyed to him that I seriously considered tying him to the back of the golf cart while I continued to play, evoking scenes from the movie *Weekend at Bernie's*. I reconsidered after realizing that I would have to explain the situation to his wife and it probably wouldn't be worth it. I thanked him for having me publicly humiliated and permanently banned from Flanders Valley Golf Course. I proceeded to tell him all the events that had occurred after he passed out on the golf course. Ken, even in his ambulatory state, responded to my saga with uncontrolled laughter. So much so, that the attending physician came running over to Ken's bedside. He looked at me sternly and said, "What are you trying to do, give this man a heart attack?" (The doctor had a good sense of humor).

In any event, the doctor said that Ken had blockage in one artery. He had suffered a heart attack and it was fortunate that he had arrived at the hospital so quickly. If the staff at Flanders Valley, paramedics, and of course the golfers who lent us their golf cart hadn't moved quickly, Ken might have sustained permanent damage. I am happy to report that Ken had a stent placed in his pulmonary artery, and like many heart attack victims, physically he is in better shape today than he was prior to his stroke. He is once again free to be the scourge of golf superintendents everywhere.

CHAPTER 12
Women Respond

You can make a good argument that this book has examined retirement from a male's perspective. However, in today's world, more and more women are working full and part time. In a significant number of cases, they are the prime bread winners whether they are single or married. The women who are married to retired spouses truly hold the key to determine if their spouse is going to embrace retirement or beg his boss to let him return to work. Realizing that the book was missing the female touch and would make it less than complete, I contemplated traveling to Scandinavia to get a sex change operation. Fortunately, I opted for a far less invasive solution to the problem.

I interviewed three Baby Boomer women who filled out questionnaires and gave me input on how retirement impacted or will impact them. The three respondents have experienced or will experience retirement from different perspectives. The first person to step up to the plate was my wife. Why? It was her idea to include this chapter, and also I enjoy an occasional home cooked meal and having my laundry done. In the spirit of objectivity, I must point out that my wife believes and has verbalized to me on occasions too numerous to count that she has worked twenty-four hours a day, seven days a week for the thirty-two years that we have been married. Due to her heavy work schedule both on the job and on the domestic front, and lack of support from her spouse, she believes that she will never be able to truly retire. Based on her intimate knowledge of the author, and potentially her prejudicial view of retirement, I will treat her as a hostile questionnaire respondent (until I read her answers), and also reserve the right to re-interview her to contradict the mistruths and inflammatory attacks that she surely will try to launch against me.

Name: Ethel Paciello

Age: 56

Education: BA in Elementary Education

Family Status: Married, three children (29, 26 and 25).

Work History: 1997 to present: Substitute teacher, Mount Olive Middle School

HOW HAS LIFE CHANGED FOR YOU WHEN YOUR SPOUSE RETIRED?

Initially there was an adjustment period. I would be rushing to get ready for work and my husband would be engaging me in conversation. When I returned from work, I would be lying if I said that the sight of my husband stretched out on the couch didn't irritate me. I didn't expect him to do house work, but I was disappointed at how little he had accomplished during the course of the day. On those rare occasions when I wasn't working, it was a definite adjustment period to have Pat at home. You don't realize how set in your ways you are. Daily living has a certain rhythm, and when the rhythm is interrupted or changed it makes you feel uncomfortable. At the onset of retirement, I looked forward to Pat's golf days. It gave me my solitude back and I felt that I was queen of my castle again. As time passed I got used to the change in our life style and adjusted to it.

WHAT HAVE BEEN THE BEST AND WORST PARTS FOR YOU WHEN YOUR SPOUSE RETIRED?

Having the ability to take numerous vacations and doing extensive travel has been a highlight for me. Spending the winter in Florida and utilizing our time-share weeks has been terrific. Many times when we are on vacation it is just Pat and I. It's good to know that after all these years we still enjoy each other's company. He still plays golf, but when he returns we have time at the pool, go see the sights, or just have a meal (reservations of course!). The worst part of retirement for me is worrying whether we have enough money to maintain our lifestyle.

WHAT HAS BEEN YOUR BIGGEST SURPRISE RELATED TO YOUR SPOUSE'S RETIREMENT?

I would like to say that my biggest surprise would be that my husband is never bored. However, knowing him as I do, that really never entered my mind. He probably is the only person that I know who truly is good at doing nothing and yet is busy! Undoubtedly, Pat's writing this book has been a pleasant surprise. It has provided conversation and laughter for family and friends and may help to explain why grandpa is so wacky to our future grand children.

WHAT IS YOUR FEELING ABOUT YOUR OWN RETIREMENT?

As a woman, I do not feel that I will ever be able to retire, especially with Pat as my husband. I can't see Pat ever taking over my laundry, cleaning, or cooking chores. Those are the things that I would like to retire from. There are a hundred different things that I do every week that no one even notices. You don't get a lot of credit for your domestic accomplishments. Mysteriously, Pat and my children put their laundry in the hamper and voila! The next day their clothing is cleaned and ironed; or they come home for dinner hungry and amazingly, a hot meal is waiting for them. I love my job as a substitute teacher at the Mount Olive Middle School. I view my work as the focal point for my daily activities. I have the best of both worlds. For the most part, I work every day, but I can take time off for vacations and not feel guilty about it.

WHAT ADVICE WOULD YOU GIVE TO WOMEN WHOSE HUSBANDS ARE ABOUT TO RETIRE?

Stop them! Keep them working! Seriously, retirement is wonderful. It is certainly deserved after working hard for many years. If you are still working, it does take time to accept your husband being home. Relax; you will get used to it. Keep doing the things that you enjoy. Above all else make sure that you have your own television set. The divorce rate for retired couples owning only one TV has to be one hundred percent. Don't expect extra help at home, but should you get it I will envy you. Lastly, make sure you laugh! It's the best medicine to promote a successful marriage.

The next person to offer some insight on the subject is Jane Cooper, a friend and neighbor. Jane has made her mark both in the business world as an entrepreneur and small business owner, and in the academic arena as a university professor. Both she, and her husband Don are closing in on retirement. The following are Jane's comments:

Name: Jane Cooper

Age: 55

Education: MA in Industrial/Organizational Psychology

Family Status: Married, two children (29 and 26).

Work History: 1998 to Present: Fairleigh Dickinson University, Professor

Courses taught: Statistics, Experimental Methods, Career Counseling, Industrial Psychology, Sports Psychology

1984 to 1998: J&J Personnel Consultants, Inc., President/Owner

Personnel Consulting Corporation. Services included: career counseling, resume writing, permanent and temporary employment agency

HOW MUCH RETIREMENT PLANNING HAVE YOU AND YOUR HUSBAND DONE?

My husband and I have been discussing retirement for the past 3 or 4 years. While we are working, we have secured a second home in California to use as a winter home when we do retire. We have invested in IRAs, 401K plans, annuities and other retirement vehicles to secure our future.

WHAT DOES RETIREMENT MEAN TO YOU?

Retirement means leaving a full-time job/career and spending more time involved in leisure activities. It does not mean retiring from life, simply from the every day responsibilities of organized work.

WHAT SPECIFIC CHANGES HAVE YOU MADE IN YOUR LIFESTYLE, OCCUPATION, ETC. TO PREPARE FOR RETIREMENT?

I'm not certain I have made any specific changes in my lifestyle other than buying a second home. My position at the university allows me to work until well past the traditional retirement age. I believe I can teach until I am in my 70s. So, regarding my current position I really don't have to "wind down."

WHEN DO YOU PLAN TO RETIRE?

I will most likely retire from my present position as a university professor when my husband retires from his job. He is 7 years older than I am, therefore his window of continuing in his current position is smaller than mine. So I want to say we can look forward to retiring within the next couple of years.

ONCE YOU STOP WORKING, HOW DO YOU PLAN TO SPEND YOUR RETIREMENT?

I plan to spend my retirement in a myriad of ways. The first is not to plan at all! I will look forward to sitting down and reading when I want to, playing golf when I want to, not just on the weekends. I enjoy dancing and would like to continue with dance lessons. In addition, I want to take painting courses. I have always volunteered my time in one way or another and would like to continue, whether it be mentoring at the juvenile detention center or delivering meals to the infirmed. I know I will need to be involved in a serious way for some cause because I don't know how to sit still! As I stated before, I will not retire from life. I will retire from my present position so my husband and I can spend significant time during the winter months in our California home. We also enjoy traveling and would like to spend more than a week at a time in Europe or Asia or Canada.

DO YOU HAVE ANY ADVICE FOR YOUNGER CAREER WOMEN AS IT RELATES TO RETIREMENT?

I believe we all have to plan for our retirement and recognize that before we know it, it's here! 401K plans are great; sock away as much as possible. Although it seems like you can't live with any less take-home pay—find a way! You can never have enough money upon retirement. Also, engage in a career before you retire that you can use after you retire. In other words, make your career not only your vocation but your avocation as well so you can continue to consult in the area because you are passionate about it. And be independent. Do not live vicariously through your children or your husband. Remember that you are an individual, not just someone's mother or wife. The more independent you are prior to retirement, the more you can focus on what is important to you after you retire. Once you reach the age of retirement it may be too late to establish yourself.

WHAT SCARES OR CONCERNS YOU ABOUT IMPENDING RETIREMENT?

The only fear I have of retiring is not earning the respect from others that I need. Most of us identify with our professions. Rarely do we earn respect as someone's mother or wife; we earn respect and develop much of our self-esteem from success outside the home (once we are adults), success defined in this context as objective accomplishments. So once I retire I am concerned that I won't have as many opportunities to "show what I am worth" and earn the respect from those who are not connected by blood or marriage (although that respect is the greatest kind). But honestly, as long as I remain healthy and can be active in body and mind, retirement will provide opportunities and challenges that I will embrace.

Judy Cooperman was kind enough to contribute to this chapter. I had never spoken or met Judy prior to doing research for this book, but once I became aware of her story I felt that Judy brought a unique perspective on retirement from a woman's point of view. Judy's journey has included a twenty-six year career as an executive in the banking profession, a successful survivor of breast cancer, and now the proud owner of a karate school. The following are Judy's thoughts on the subject:

NAME: Judy Cooperman

AGE: 51

EDUCATION: B.A. Economics, Georgia State University

FAMILY STATUS: Married, three children (25, 20, and 11).

WORK HISTORY: 2005 to the present, President / Owner of Shido-kan Karate of Mahwah

2003-2005 PNC Advisors, Senior Client Advisor and Director of Woman's Financial Services Network.

1998-2003 Citigroup Private Bank, Business Development Director

1993-1998 First Union National Bank, Managing Director, Private Client Group

1989-1993 Citibank Private Bank, Vice-President, Private Banker

1976-1989 several positions in both the banking and AIESEC, an international not-for-profit organization

HOW MUCH RETIREMENT PLANNING HAVE YOU AND YOUR HUSBAND DONE?

My husband and I both share a passion for the martial arts, but we never imagined that we would own a karate school; However, four years ago a shopping center opened near our townhouse community which sparked an idea that got us thinking about just that. Since Mitchell had earned his 4th Degree Black Belt around that time, he became eligible within our karate association to own a school, so we began to talk about it as a retirement planning strategy and a way for me to leave my banking career. About two years later, another shopping center adjacent to the existing one was soon to be under construction and we had done enough pre-planning to contact the builder to enter into lease negotiations. Owning our own business and planning our retirement strategy soon became a reality and our school officially opened January 24, 2005.

As a private banker for many years, I assisted my clients with their wealth management needs, and it became routine for me to consider my own investments and retirement planning. As the primary breadwinner in both my first and second marriages, I have been responsible for managing household bills, insurance, investments, and pension assets for almost three decades. However, we decided to complete a retirement plan in 2004 with an outside financial advisor to get an up-to-date projection taking into consideration the money we would be spending on starting up the karate school. We projected at the time that I would be working for five more years until 55, and that my husband would work at least another ten years in our financial services professions, and we conservatively projected that there would be no revenue coming in from our soon to be opened karate school. The thought was that the school would provide extra income and an enjoyable livelihood during our future retirement years.

When the karate school broke even in the fifth month, we knew that we would be able to count on income from the karate school in the near future and decided it was time to really focus on the school full-time to get it profitable as fast as possible. Thus, I decided to leave my 26 year banking career to run my own business, spend more time with my family, enjoy my hobbies, and have much less stress in my life. The decision was not a painful or difficult one because I had done enough thinking and planning, and it seemed that everything leading up to this decision was meant to be. Little pieces of the puzzle fell into place naturally. Since I am still young enough to reenter the workforce, I decided to focus on the journey rather than the destination. In many ways, this new chapter in my life is full of more adventure than I could have imagined it would be.

WHAT DOES RETIREMENT MEAN TO YOU?

Retirement does not necessarily mean not working, but it means not working for someone else any longer. I have always wanted to own and operate my own business, and my goal was to retire at 55 from banking and then start a business. The business got started earlier than planned, and its initial success has given me the confidence to leave salaried employment sooner than expected. It also means that I have much more flexibility in scheduling my hobbies, doing errands, and running our household. This means more relaxation, less frustration, less stress, and more time for myself, including sleeping and doing absolutely nothing if I want.

WHAT SPECIFIC CHANGES HAVE YOU MADE IN YOUR LIFE STYLE, OCCUPATION, ETC. TO PREPARE FOR RETIREMENT?

Prior to leaving my job, we refinanced our townhouse to consolidate a first mortgage. We used the home equity line of credit to build the karate school and pay off outstanding credit card balances.

We are more cautious about spending money on anything that is not absolutely needed, including reducing our lunches and dinners out. We have eliminated our cleaning service, and have asked our children to take on more responsibility for some expenses which we had been covering for them.

DO YOU HAVE ANY ADVICE FOR YOUNGER CAREER WOMEN AS IT RELATES TO RETIREMENT?

Don't depend on anyone else, whether it's family or a spouse, to plan for your future. Use your own skills, abilities and motivation to reach your goals. If you get some help along the way, that's great, but don't rely on it or count on it. Save early in life, save regularly, use investment discipline, and build skills you might use for creating future self-employment income. This is the best advice I can give someone.

From the time I began working, I always saved at least 10% of my gross earnings, and tried to put that money in tax-deferred investments such as a 401K plan and/or IRA accounts. I also took advantage of other opportunities presented by my employers, such as employee stock options plans, which for me always resulted in long-term capital growth far beyond what I could have gotten in most mutual funds. I regularly review my 401K investment selections, and opted for more aggressive investments (small and mid-cap, international) for most of my career. Making reallocations and rebalancing yearly has also helped me to manage risks and improve returns. If you don't know about asset allocation, ask for help. Even though I went through a divorce and lost half of my investments when I was 40 years old (17 years into my banking career) I stayed the course and it has served me well. Live below your means so you can be disciplined about saving.

Because I did not have any inherited wealth and got no financial support from my family, I purposely chose a career which would give me the opportunity to earn a pension that I could count on. Of course, as I ended up in several different companies, I did not earn a pension for all the years I worked, but I did have 401K income and stock options, etc., that helped.

If you are fortunate to have a profession that you can leverage now or in the future for self-employment income, you will have a better opportunity to enhance revenue potential, and build a second career during retirement. I never actually realized that my skills in the martial arts, which for most of my life was a personal interest or hobby, would enable me to start my own business. This perhaps has been the greatest surprise and reward of my life and what has enabled me to leave my traditional banking career behind earlier than expected.

Being happy and enjoying what you do with your life is more important than staying in a job or career just for the "pension". If we are disciplined about saving and investing, we can take more risks along the way. The idea of working with one company or staying in one field of work your whole life just for the retirement benefits often limits one's true potential and opportunities. I would encourage younger women not to have pre-conceived notions about retirement, but to remain open and flexible to opportunities that present themselves, even if it means taking risks, especially early in their careers. One door closes and another opens, and we find new paths that lead in new directions all the time.

HOW HAS YOUR "NEW RETIREMENT" IM-PACTED YOUR FAMILY RELATIONSHIPS, FINANCIAL STRATEGIES, AND YOUR OUTLOOK ON LIFE?

My new retirement has meant giving up a regular paycheck and relying upon my savings to meet our monthly expenses not covered by my husband's income. I say my savings because these are investments in my name which I earned prior to this second marriage. Thus, it was very much my decision to retire from my banking career. I did not want to dip into my retirement assets until age 60 at the earliest, so we are having to look at our expenses much more carefully than ever before. Being cautious about eating out and cutting back on gifts and unnecessary expenses is not easy for me or my husband, so we are looking at living within a budget, something that is new for us. We have stopped being as generous with our grown daughter (age 25, now married with a child) because of our new budget, and some of our donations will no doubt be cut back until our business generates more revenue. We are trying to sell our boat, which we really don't use that often, and have already sold one of our two classic cars (a 1966 Mustang). However, we still have our 1963 Merc which we enjoy taking to the car shows.

My outlook on life is positive, and I feel as though I am beginning a new journey with no idea where it is taking me.

That is a very liberating feeling, and very exciting. I know that I have choices, and for the first time in my life I feel like I am making choices rather than feeling pushed into them. I enjoy being able to structure my day around myself rather than around my employer. I don't know what tomorrow will bring. Perhaps the karate school will become incredibly successful sooner then we think and I will hire someone to relieve me of some of the business operations, thus creating more opportunities for me to pursue other interests. I may need to go back to work for someone else if the karate school does not generate sufficient income for us, but I'll cross that bridge when I get there. At that time, I might pursue something on a part-time basis.

For now, I am less stressed, more relaxed, more creative in my personal life than ever before. If this is the beginning of a new journey, I couldn't be better set to enjoy it than I am right now. I feel as if there is more focus on me and my family than ever before: eating right, exercising, sleeping more, going to the pool, gardening, enjoying seeing my grandson, and building our "own" business. On my refrigerator, I have a quotable magnet that serves as an inspiration for me from the late comedian Gilda Radner. I think her message could be applicable to my "new retirement":

"Some stories don't have a clear beginning, middle, and end. Life is about not knowing, having to change, taking the moment and making the best of it, without knowing what's going to happen next. Delicious ambiguity..."

In addition to the three respondents to my questionnaire, I spoke to many female Baby Boomers about retirement. As with any large group of people being polled there was a variety of answers to my questions. However, certain patterns seemed to repeat themselves. Based on their responses, these are a few of my observations on the subject.

By and large, a woman's attitude toward retirement was greatly influenced by her occupational status. If a woman had been a stay-at-home mom for the bulk of her life, the responses showed that she wanted to continue with that life style, substituting more social activities in lieu of domestic chores and parenting. If the woman was employed in the work force for a substantial amount of years, she was not nearly as motivated to leave the occupation and embrace retirement. The woman who worked part-time or did volunteer work prior to retirement wanted to continue in that capacity. In essence, Newton's first law of motion proves in this case to be applicable. A body at rest tends to stay at rest, while a body in motion tends to stay in motion, traveling at a constant speed and in a straight line until acted upon by an outside force. (I knew that high school physics would some day come in handy.)

I think that comparing Baby Boomer women to Baby Boomer men in the work place is an interesting contrast. Men, by and large, are discussing and planning their retirement strategy years before retirement becomes a reality. Many women raised and nurtured their families and then either started or resumed their careers. They are still trying to move up the ladder of success while many of their male counterparts are in a holding pattern. Or to fracture a 60's slogan, the women are dropping in and the men are dropping out. Whether it is the financial independence that working women have achieved, the feeling of accomplishment outside the home, or the stimulation of a new social environment, in general working Baby Boomer women are happy to continue in their chosen professions.

The one vocation where my observations did not hold water is the female dominated teaching profession. I found grade school teachers to be very similar to males in the work place, in that they plan and calculate their retirement strategy.

They utilize their retirement formula and determine when they can financially afford to retire, and when the numbers make sense, they say *adios* to the teaching profession. One can hypothesize that teachers eager to retire are influenced by their generous retirement package, but it is also obvious that job satisfaction for many reasons (which are too complex to discuss here) declines as the years roll on.

SO LET'S COMPARE BABY BOOMER WOMEN AND MEN AND DETERMINE WHO HAS CONTRIBUTED MORE TO THE SUCCESSFUL PLANNING AND ACHIEVEMENT OF RETIREMENT GOALS:

Tale of the Tape

1. Men are inherently lazy
2. Men do one thing at a time. They do it well and see the project to completion.
3. Men want to play golf, drink beer, and watch sports.
4. Men want to save for retirement as long as number three is not affected.

1. Women are far more motivated.
2. Women are exceptional at multitasking. (See raising a family, managing a home, and being gainfully employed).
3. Women don't want to play golf, drink beer, and watch sports. They consider these things a waste of time and money.
4. Women will save for luxury items like the children's college education, food, and shelter.

The judge's verdict is in. It's a unanimous decision! Baby Boomer women are far more valuable to their family, the work place, and keeping their husbands on the straight and narrow path. Shame on you men who bring so little to the table as retirement beckons. Your punishment is to spend the end of your days banished to hang out with your friends pursuing worthless leisure time activities and repeating phrases like, "Yes, dear," and "You're right, honey," right before you exit the house and go off to play. Men, you are pathetic! You deserve your cruel fate.

CHAPTER 13
Retired Boomers

I interviewed four friends who are retired Baby Boomers. I asked them to fill out a questionnaire and provide additional information that they deemed relevant to the subject matter. In keeping with the spirit of the book, I will highlight their backgrounds and recount some of the experiences that we have shared.

Shelley Kaufman is a boyhood friend from the same neighborhood in the Bronx. After high school, we lost touch. Many years later, our mothers ran into one another on the subway in New York City. As mothers are wont to do, they both bragged about their wonderful sons and how well they were doing. It turned out that Shelley and I were living in neighboring towns ten minutes from one another. My wife was planning a surprise 40th birthday party for me and to throw me off the track, which is a fairly simple assignment, she suggested that we go to dinner with Shelley and his wife, Patty. I had spoken to Shelley on the phone, but we had not been able to get together. I looked forward to meeting a friend from my youth and had no idea that this was a ruse to get me out of the house while the guests filtered into the party.

On Saturday, Shelley and his wife arrived at our house. He looked in great shape. He was a good athlete as a child and possessed very good foot speed. He billed himself as the world's fastest Jew. Realistically, he probably was the fastest Jewish guy in our neighborhood. What really impressed me though was when Shelley told me that he recently had just retired from Wall Street and had no inclination to continue working full-time on Wall Street or any place else. Shelley had arrived at the destination that I was always dreaming about. My wife, Ethel, reminded Shelley about his mission. "I'm going to tell Pat to go to the store to pick up bread and milk before we supposedly go out to dinner. You volunteer to drive and keep him out of the house for as long as possible."

Shelley played his part perfectly and off we went to the store. After not seeing someone for over 20+ years, we both had a ton of questions for each other. Shelley proceeded to drive to the store about ten minutes away. We got on the highway and Shelley was going about 25 miles per hour when the speed limit was 50 miles per hour and there was not a lot of traffic! What traffic there was, was blowing their horns at us. Shelley is hunched over the steering wheel. His forehead almost touched the dashboard. He reminded me of Artie Johnson from *Laugh In* pedaling on his tricycle. Shelley saw the look of horror on my face and tried to allay my fears. "Don't worry, Pat. I can't see very well at night so I drive very cautiously." I thought to myself, "Cautiously! I could jog to the store faster than you could drive. What a shame my boyhood friend had become Methuselah. Maybe this retirement thing wasn't all it was cracked up to be." I tried to put a positive spin on the situation and be empathetic to Shelley's plight. "These roads are very tricky around here and they don't have lights on the highways like they used to. Why don't I drive and you can take it easy." "No, no," Shelly insisted, "Thanks, but I can do this. Keep the faith, Pat."

He continued on at his slow as molasses pace and we finally arrived at the store. I instructed Shelley to turn off at the exit.

He looked puzzled. "Which exit?" "The next one," I replied, with a twinge of sarcasm. "Which next one?" he mumbled. "Are you kidding me?" I thought. "This guy is either brain dead or I am in the middle of an Abbot and Costello routine." Amazingly, for the first time on our journey, he punches the accelerator and we speed past the exit. I wanted to strangle Shelley on the spot. He turns to me apologetically and says he doesn't perform well under pressure. By this point, I was a beaten man. We eventually arrive at the store and return home. I just wanted to get the night over with and chalk it up to a bad experience. I opened the door and I was greeted with a chorus of "Happy Birthday" from friends. Shelley came over to me and declared that he was not a mental case. He explained to me that his role in this deception was to keep me out of the house for as long as possible. I told him he deserved an Oscar for his memorable performance.

The following is Shelley's response to the retirement questionnaire.

Age: 56

Education: B.S. Mathematics at the Polytechnic Institute of Brooklyn 1965-1969 (Cum Laude)

Completed course work for MBA in Finance

Retired: May, 1989

HOW WERE YOU ABLE TO AFFORD TO RETIRE EARLY? (HOW DID YOU ACQUIRE YOUR WEALTH?)

I was a principal in the Arbitrage Department of PaineWebber. As such, I earned a percentage of the profits that the department was able to generate. We were able to earn substantial revenues for the firm, and the distribution of these revenues to our department was sufficient to allow me to retire very early.

WHAT DO YOU DO NOW THAT YOU NO LONGER HAVE A TRADITIONAL JOB?

Immediately after retiring, I became very active in the activities of my two sons and my daughter. For several years, I coached virtually every baseball, soccer, basketball, and softball team any of them was involved with. Right now, I spend three or four afternoons at a health club, working out and playing racquetball. I read a lot and spend a fair amount of time on the computer. I have become active in conservative politics. On the other side of the coin, my wife and I are volunteer tutors at The Neighborhood House in Morristown, New Jersey.

Although I am really not much of a traveler, we have spent time in Italy, Spain, and Portugal over the last few years. Of course, I do spend a fair amount of time monitoring my investments. I am primarily interested in staying retired.

DO YOU MISS "WORKING?"

I definitely miss the challenge of competing, day in and day out, against the best and brightest minds on Wall Street. I don't miss the toll that the stress was taking on my body. The commute from Morris County, New Jersey to midtown New York, which averaged two hours a day in each direction, is what I miss the least.

THE BEST AND WORST PART OF RETIREMENT

The simple act of not having to wake up in the morning and hurry off to work is probably the best part. It's the same feeling one would get on Saturday morning or as a kid on the first day of Christmas vacation. The worst part is probably the loss of the income. I am very organized in the area of finances and I certainly would not have retired at such an early age if I had not been able to afford it. Nevertheless, the fact that I am now living off of my accumulated assets, rather than the current sweat of my brow has obviously caused me to scale down my lifestyle somewhat. I have been fortunate enough to help my children acquire an education and back them to a degree in their purchase of homes, but my contributions have been somewhat limited by the fact that my income is now fixed and at a reduced level.

WHAT RECOMMENDATIONS DO YOU HAVE FOR BOOMERS CONSIDERING RETIREMENT?

The biggest fear that most of my friends have is that they will be bored after leaving the job world. Nothing could be further from the truth! The more common statement I have been hearing from those who have retired is, "I am so busy now, I wonder how I ever had time to work." Even people who never had any real hobbies or specific interests have found that the very fact that they don't have 40-60 hours per week tied up in working and commuting opens up huge vistas to explore. People forget that this is the only life that we are given. It is far better to scale down a bit (or even a lot) than to work for so long that there will be little time to enjoy oneself at the end. As the old saying goes, "Nobody ever had an epitaph that read: 'He's sorry he didn't spend more time at the office.'"

HAVE YOU MADE ANY LIFESTYLE CHANGES SINCE YOU RETIRED?

I never really was a huge spendthrift when I was working, so the lifestyle changes were minimal. I wasn't interested in spending my entire income while I was employed. I probably was living (fairly comfortably) on less than half of what I was earning. By putting a sizable amount of money into a savings plan and not having a desire for big ticket items, (i.e., expensive cars, vacation homes, boats, etc.) the transition into retirement mode was less volatile.

HAVE YOU MADE ANY CHANGES IN OTHER

AREAS, (I.E., INVESTING, FINANCIAL, INSURANCE, LEGAL, ETC.?)

My investment strategy has evolved naturally, as it should for all people as they age. Growth stocks are fine for the younger investor and they become growth & income stocks for the middle-aged, and finally, income stocks for the older investor. Whether your investments are in stocks, bonds, or real estate, the time to take risks is when you are young. At this point in my life, I am not interested in doubling my assets, but merely in keeping what I have so that I won't have to get up in the morning and go to work.

The next person to share his retirement experiences was my college roommate Dennis Textor. We shared a small room at our fraternity house in Palisades Park, New Jersey. Dennis had only spent two years at college when he decided to get married, join the real world, and get a job. Most of the brothers felt sorry for Dennis. How was he going to make a good living without a college education? Why would he forfeit two years of beer blasts, partying and alcohol-induced nirvana? For most of us, marriage, starting a career, and getting drafted were three things to delay as long as possible.

Dennis joined the police force and worked his way up the organization. He was a detective for the Bergen County Prosecutor's Office and eventually finished his career as an assistant Police Chief. When he retired from the force at 49 years of age, he was the first fraternity brother from our age group to retire. We did have many fraternity brothers who did not work for long stretches of time prior to Dennis' retirement. However, I carefully pointed out to these individuals that unemployment and retirement are not two words which share the exact meaning.

When we lived together in our fraternity house, our

diminutive room was divided by a tattered gossamer cloth that could be stretched to give the illusion, make that delusion, that one could have some privacy when either one of us would have a female visitor staying overnight (which was somewhat of a rare occurrence). Yet, when Dennis and I socialize these days and reminisce about our fraternity times, we recall those sleepovers with fondness, although the frequency seems to have increased as we have gotten older. We would pull the curtain closed so our guest would have the feeling of being in a separate room and the roommate who was alone could continue to sleep.

The divider was so threadbare that most girls didn't believe there was a divider. They then wanted proof, in my case, that Dennis was asleep. Here I was faced with a difficult dilemma. Dennis sleeps with one eye open! This is a very eerie sight for the uninitiated and didn't bolster my case for complete privacy. My powers of persuasion had to be at their sharpest, but I realized that a winning argument would be generously rewarded. I would take my guest to the other side of the curtain, a distance of about three feet, and in hushed whispers begin to start my experiments to prove that Dennis was truly asleep and oblivious to anything that was taking place or about to take place in our room. I pretended to poke out his eye with a sharpened pencil and blinded his open eye with the beam of a flash light. Dennis did not blink, and made no response; finally, victory. I had seized the day!

The morning after was always interesting, especially those times when Dennis was not really asleep the night before and proceeded to parrot back to me all the desperate lines I had uttered the previous evening.

The following is Dennis' response to the questionnaire.

Age: 53

Education: Associates Degree (102 credits)

Retired: September, 1999

HOW WERE YOU ABLE TO AFFORD TO RETIRE EARLY? (HOW DID YOU ACQUIRE YOUR WEALTH?)

I couldn't afford NOT to retire! I was in a pretty unique situation. With deductions coming out of my paycheck for Social Security, Union Dues, Pension Fund, etc., I actually "take home" more money—approximately $400 more a month than when I worked. That, coupled with reduced work-related expenses, such as clothes, dry cleaning, lunches and supplies, added to the increase in my monthly cash once I retired.

With three children to provide for and send through college, my investment portfolio started somewhat later in my career. Two factors that I attribute to the fast growth in acquiring my wealth were good advice and luck. The "good advice" was given to me by a senior co-worker. He talked me into joining a deferred compensation savings plan (similar to a 401K). That was in addition to our pension plan. His advice was to start out with the minimum monthly contribution (since that was all I could afford at the time). Then, every year when I received a raise, put half of the raise towards my household expenses and increase my deferred compensation contribution by the amount of the other half. That way every year you were seeing more money for expenses and not missing the extra monies going into your savings plan. Well, after a twenty-eight year career, the deferred compensation savings plan, with compounded interest, developed into a healthy sum.

The second factor, "luck," came into play when I decided to get into the stock market in the 90's—affectionately known as the "good years," when the stock market was doing so well that we all thought we were financial geniuses. Then, when the Y2K scare was approaching, I fell for the hype and pulled all my money out of the stock market and went conservative with Tax Free Municipal Bonds.

As we entered the 21st century, with no millennium disaster occurring, I became sidetracked with personal events and didn't spend the time re-investing into the stock market. I just left my money where it was, conservatively. That turned out to be lucky over the next number of years because, unfortunately, while many of my friends were seeing their stock market investments and IRA's decline, mine were still rising—although at a slower pace. It is only this year, 2004, that I have changed my portfolio allocations back to include individual stocks and mutual funds.

WHAT DO YOU DO NOW THAT YOU NO LONGER HAVE A TRADITIONAL JOB?

Immediately after retiring, I became involved as a volunteer with the American Red Cross. With the schooling that they gave me, coupled with my training in emergency situations (as a law enforcement officer), I am qualified to travel to national disaster sites and assist people in a variety of ways. This type of spontaneous service keeps alive that adrenaline rush that I have always craved. I'm fortunate that my wife, Denise, is an emergency medical technician in New Jersey and my partner when we travel to national disaster sites.

DO YOU MISS WORKING?

I do not miss working at all. This comes as quite a surprise to me because I was a cop "24/7". The type of job I had required me to be on-call 24 hours a day—often leaving bed in the middle of the night or working on extensive surveillance details. I thought I would miss that terribly, but I can honestly say I don't. In the five years that I have been retired, I've stopped by the office two times.

THE BEST AND WORST PART OF RETIRMENT?

Virtually a stress-free life is perhaps the best part of retirement. We start off most days with a leisurely breakfast, reading the daily chronicles. Five days per week, or more, we go to The Ocean Club, our gym and health spa. We are then free to do whatever we wish, which usually entails golf, boating, poker, or social invitations.

As for the second part of your question, what is the worst part? I have probably, as part of my job, interviewed over 300 applicants. One of the questions we used to ask (somewhere in the guidelines it was recommended to ask—although I don't know why) "What is your best quality and what is your worst?" Most people were never honest in giving their "worst." It was usually a made up answer, one that they thought you would buy. If I have to answer your "worst part of retirement" question, it would be a made up answer. As of yet, I have not found one bad element about retired life.

WHAT RECOMMENDATIONS DO YOU HAVE FOR BOOMERS CONSIDERING RETIREMENT?

Retire when you're ready. What I mean by that is that it has to be your decision. You have to be psychologically ready to take the right frame of mind into retirement. Don't do it because of peer or family pressure. Also, don't be afraid that people will label you as an "Old Retired Person." It is not the end, by any means, of a productive life. Retired people today are healthy, in better shape, and more active than ever before. Enjoy your family, friends, and hobbies. You'll now have time to expand on them all.

HAVE YOU MADE ANY LIFESTYLE CHANGES SINCE YOU RETIRED?

Exercise was always a hobby of mine. Now, with the available time I have, working out is more of a pleasure than just a routine. I've become more conscience of a healthy diet and have incorporated that into my lifestyle.

Financially, we are comfortably set up, allowing us to winter in Florida, cruise, and travel to countries we never had time to before.

HAVE YOU MADE ANY CHANGES IN OTHER AREAS (i.e., INVESTING, FINANCIAL, INSURANCE, LEGAL, etc.)?

I have devoted some considerable time deciding on how to organize my affairs. This trait comes from my father who was very organized. I saw how at ease that made family members feel when unfortunate circumstances arose.

Our first investment was in long-term care insurance for both my wife and me. Too many times I have seen the emotional and financial stress put on a spouse or family member due to caring for an individual with medical problems. As you can gather by now, I am not a proponent of stress. Not for me or those I care about. Long-term care insurance will help ease a stressful situation. You must do the proper research before purchasing such a policy. Don't jump at someone else's recommendations. If I never need the insurance, and I never recoup one cent from collecting on a long-term care insurance policy, it will be money well-spent. It is a win-win situation.

Other obvious legal documents should be either originated or updated, such as wills, living trusts, powers of attorney, and letters of special instructions.

Investment strategies surely change when you have reached the enjoyment of retirement life. Again, this varies with the individual. If you have a comfortable guaranteed pension coming in, such as I do, with a yearly cost of living increase adjustment, you can still afford to be somewhat adventurous with your investment portfolio.

At one time, my investments were spread amongst three brokerage firms where I kept a hands-on approach in the daily management of our finances. Now, to simplify matters, I have my portfolio managed by one company with whom I am very comfortable. I have discussed our financial strategies with them and let them mange our portfolio on a daily basis, which allows us more time to enjoy retirement life!

Batting next in the retirement line up is Dollar Bill (obviously not his real name). Dollar Bill was a friend, and a next door neighbor in a nice development in Morris County, New Jersey. The common bonds that the residents shared were that for the most of us, this was the first home that we owned. We all had young children, were thirty something in age and poured every cent we had into home ownership, which meant everyone had good jobs, but were cash poor. Bill had six children during the time that he lived in our neighborhood. It seemed his poor wife was pregnant or giving birth the entire time we were neighbors. The rumor (which I started), was that Bill was only allowed to swim in the town pool at designated times. When Bill went for a swim, all the women had to exit the pool to ensure that Bill would not mystically impregnate them. Bill took the concept of adult swim to a new level.

Bill's approach to life was diametrically opposed to my lifestyle. Or to put it in other words, he was industrious, hard-working, very focused, and I was not. For instance, I was the only person on the block who had a snow blower. I told Bill he could feel free to borrow it at any time. Bill was very appreciative of my offer. During every snow fall, he would open up my garage doors and in the wee hours of the morning, plow my driveway first and then proceed to clear the snow from his driveway. The first time he performed this task, I admonished him and told him that servicing my driveway was not necessary. He insisted and I bowed to his wishes. My free snow-blowing system continued for three years. It was a great feeling to know that you could leave your house at 9 am during blizzard conditions, jump in your car and drive off to work without worrying about your car making it out of the driveway.

Finally, I told Bill that I had to talk to him about his use of the snow blower. Bill became red-faced and apologized profusely if I thought that he was taking advantage of my generosity. I looked at him with a serious expression on my face and measured my words carefully, "Bill, I am not upset that you continue to borrow my snow blower. I am, however, a little annoyed at your snow-blowing schedule. As you know, I leave for work at 9:00 am to avoid the heavy commuter traffic. You are plowing my driveway at 6:00 in the morning. This affects my sleep patterns and makes me less effective at work. Could you please not be so selfish and work me in between 7:30 and 8:30 am?" Even though by this time Bill knew I was a trickster and a goof-off, my stern demeanor made him feel uncomfortable. Finally, I couldn't suppress my laughter any longer and proceeded to just let it go. Bill quickly realized he was a victim of a practical joke and joined me in the laugh-a-thon. However, two weeks later, he purchased his own snow blower and my snow removal service was cancelled.

My favorite Bill story really centers on Bill's wife. As the years passed, Bill became a high-powered executive in the corporate sector. He spent a tremendous amount of time traveling all over the world with his job, and when he was home, he would spend the weekends in Philadelphia to secure his Masters degree from the Wharton School at the University of Pennsylvania.

One Saturday, I was walking around the development when I came across Bill's wife. I asked her if Bill was home and she told me that once again he was out of town taking classes for his MBA. Out of nowhere, with no hesitation or pre-meditation, I launched into a police detective persona that was closely modeled after Peter Falk in the wildly successful television show, *Columbo*. I said, "Look, Sally. Can't you see what's going on here? Your husband claims he is away from home due to business travel. Nobody I know travels as much as he. Bill is still going to school? How many advanced degrees does he really need and why couldn't he find a school in New Jersey like Rutgers or Princeton, so that he would not have to disappear from his family? And what's the deal with these braces? Christ, he is thirty-nine years old and now he wants to fix his teeth? Let's face it, Sally. Your husband is having an affair. I wouldn't be surprised if he has another whole family that he shares time with." I am at the peak of this diatribe when my wife calls out to me and tells me that I have an important phone call. I tell Sally that I have to go and remind her to say hello to Bill for me. As I jog back to my house, I flash a quick grin and think to myself that was pretty funny. Bill possesses the qualities of a model boy scout, and off the cuff, I made a pretty good case for him to star in a sleazy made-for-television movie.

I went about my business for the rest of the day and my conversation with Bill's wife soon faded from my memory. At about 10:30 at night, the phone rings and I recognize Bill's voice. He is rather agitated and sounds upset. "What did you say to my wife? She thinks I am having an affair and told me to pack my bags. I asked her where she would get this crazy idea and she said you told her." I immediately sensed that Bill was giving me payback for all the jokes I had played on him over the years. I lethargically responded, "No problem. I have an extra bedroom and you will be able to walk to your wife's house to visit the kids." I then expected Bill to say something like, "Geez, Paciello, I thought for sure I had your number this time." But, instead, he unleashed a stream of words that cannot be found in Webster's Dictionary. In a flash, I realized that I had gone over the line. I felt nauseated. I apologized every way possible and offered to go to his house and explain to his wife that I was only kidding. He told me that I had done enough damage for one day and to be invisible for the next few days while he patched everything up with Sally. I went into a self-imposed witness protection program for safety. I eventually sent Sally flowers and soon all was forgiven.

A few months later, Bill and I were playing golf and almost immediately this incident was recounted. Once again, I expressed my deepest apologies, but I couldn't resist asking Bill, "Now that time has passed and there was no concrete damage, can't you see the humor in all of this?" He laughed, flipped my golf ball in the pond, and I knew we were all good.

The following is Dollar Bill's response to the questionnaire.

Age: 53

Education: MBA, The Wharton School, University of Pennsylvania

Masters in Engineering Administration, The University of Utah

B.S. in Electrical Engineering, Stevens Institute of Technology

Retired: October, 2003

HOW WERE YOU ABLE TO AFFORD TO RETIRE EARLY? (HOW DID YOU ACQUIRE YOUR WEALTH?)

Early retirement came with a little planning and a lot of luck. Until I moved to Massachusetts, I was doing well with a solid six-figure income which enabled me to send my children to college and afford a comfortable lifestyle. My annual salary was complemented by the sale of stock options, which I had accumulated over the years with Hewlett Packard. My job afforded me a comfortable life, but not enough to retire. When I moved to Massachusetts, Hewlett Packard divested all of the non-computer related businesses and my business (Medical) was spun out into a publicly traded company called Agilent Technologies. Very soon after the spin out, Agilent decided to sell the Medical business and approached me and the other four general managers to help sell the business. I worked with investment bankers, attorneys, and the Department of Justice to sell the business to Philips Electronics. Philips purchased the business and took ownership in August of 2001.

During this period of time, Agilent gave me a significant bonus to help with the sale, and Philips gave me a significant 2-year contract to remain with Philips after the sale. Philips wanted me to stay after the 2-year contract had expired, but I decided to retire and return to New Jersey. I had established certain financial goals which would give me the opportunity to retire and these two events helped me to reach my goals. In a sense, these last five years of my working life support the idea of "being in the right place at the right time."

WHAT DO YOU DO NOW THAT YOU NO LONGER HAVE A TRADITIONAL JOB?

Over the years, I have listened to many people who have retired (some early and some at the more traditional age). These people taught me a lot about how to prepare for retirement, especially if you desire to retire when you are in your 50's. One lesson that I learned that was repeated by many individuals is that "something that you enjoy and do infrequently when you are working may not be as much fun when you can do it all the time." For example, I had a relative who loved to play golf and usually played twice a month while he was working. His dream was to retire and play golf everyday. When he retired at 56, he moved to Florida and began playing golf every day. Even though he enjoyed the game, playing golf every day soon became unsatisfying. The big lesson here is to ensure that you have many diverse interests which you can enjoy. They should also include some interests which challenge you mentally, physically, and emotionally.

With that said, I wanted to ensure that I would have a number of things to do which would keep me challenged, entertained and keep life fun! All my life I enjoyed working around the house. I like to do carpentry, woodworking, painting, wallpapering, landscaping, etc. Over the years, I have rebuilt three complete homes, built a number of decks, and finished basements. I enjoy playing golf although I am not a good golfer. Unfortunately, I had only been able to play about 6 times each year when I was working. During the last 10 to 15 years of my career, I traveled extensively (as much as 50% of my time). Each year, I would make three or four trips to Europe, three or four trips to Asia, and eight to ten trips within the United States. As you can imagine, this kept me away from home and separated me from my family during the year. My family enjoys the beach and we had a home at the Jersey shore many years ago, but sold it in the early 1990's.

Considering all of the above, I have spent the majority of the past year doing the following:

- I cancelled my lawn service so I now mow my own lawn and do all of the outside landscaping and maintenance. We are going to put new paved walkways and stone walls around the house.
- I maintain my swimming pool.
- I decided to remodel our home. Our home is 18 years

old and we are going through the house room-by-room. We are putting new wood moldings throughout the house, changing wallpaper/paint, installing new wood floors and changing furniture. Since our home has 14 rooms and a basement, this will keep us busy for quite some time.

- I try to play golf 2 to 3 times each week. Not only do I enjoy the sport, but my 18-year-old son is an excellent golfer and this allows us to spend time together (as long as he continues to tolerate my golf mediocrity).

- My wife was not able to travel with me on business trips since she had to maintain the household and care for our six children. We have made a couple of 3 or 4 day trips during this past year and will continue to do so each year.

- After I retired, we purchased a home at the Jersey shore and we spend a lot of time there. As families mature and children grow older, it becomes more difficult to spend time together. One of the reasons I purchased the shore home was to use it as a gathering focal point for our family so that we can spend more time together. This is important to me since my job took me away from them for quite some time.

- The shore home is relatively new (six years old) but the maintenance and slight modifications we plan will keep me busy.

- I enjoy reading all types of books. During my business career, I spent many hours each week reading reports, journals and business briefs. I had very little time for personal reading except when I was on a business trip and even then it was limited. I have started reading books again and will try to at least read one book each month.

DO YOU MISS WORKING?

There are a number of things that I miss about my job. Most of the positions that I had during the past 26 years in industry revolved around transforming or turning around a department or business. The General Manager positions that I had, offered unique challenges. The first centered on turning a business around from decreasing sales and lack of profitability to growth and high profit levels. The next GM position revolved around changing the product and business strategy to meet the changing market needs and technology trends. The final GM position focused on transitioning the business to a new owner, integrating our business into a larger medical division within the company and maintaining customers who are traditionally very loyal to product brands or companies. I miss the business challenges, interacting with employees/customers and defining business/product strategies to beat the competition. In certain aspects, I miss the worldwide travel which brought me to many countries and cities and allowed me to see many sights which most people will never have the chance to see (i.e., the Great Wall of China, the remains of the Berlin Wall, the ancient cities of Spain and Italy).

WHAT IS THE BEST AND WORST PART OF RETIREMENT?

Best: Spending more time with family.

Not feeling like I am constantly trading off business needs with family needs. Business needs usually won!

I am able to enjoy retirement while I am still young and healthy.

Having the resources to do what I want to do (within reason) and still provide a good life for my family.

Re-establish ties with friends and spend more time with them.

Worst: A struggle to keep up with technology. Now I know why some retirees are not computer literate.

It was a tough choice to walk away from a career that you worked hard to establish and became very financially rewarding. At my last position, I was making between six and seven figures each year. When I talk to coworkers my age who are still with the company it reminds me of the financial rewards people at my level receive.

The experience which made this choice easier for me was a lesson that I learned from a person whom I respect and admire. He worked very hard all of his life and made many personal and family sacrifices for his career. He had a wife and 3 grown children whom he did not see very often due to his business travels and the fact that they lived 2000 miles away. He had the financial ability to retire at 55, but chose to remain for 2 to 3 more years.

After 3 years, he retired and joined his family. Within 3 years after his retirement, two of his young sons (in their mid to late 20's) died accidentally. He had more than enough money to retire at 55, but did not do so.

I visited with him after his second son had passed away. He gave me this advice. "I had enough money for two lifetimes when I was 55, but chose not to retire thinking I had time to spend with my family. I gave up three years with my family to gain more money, which I will probably not spend in my lifetime. It was not the right choice. When you can, be sure to put your family first above all else since you do not know what the future or fate will present."

Lessons like this one are very precious and reinforce the

notion that you can learn a lot from your elders if you take the time to listen, talk, and appreciate their lifelong experience.

WHAT RECOMMENDATIONS DO YOU HAVE FOR BOOMERS CONSIDERING RETIREMENT?

First of all, create a business plan for your retirement just as you would for your business. Decide what lifestyle you want to maintain after retirement, what you are willing to give up and what you want to continue to do. This will form the foundation for the financial plan/goals you will need to meet to support your desires.

Next, develop a step-by-step action plan to reach your financial goals so that you can measure your progress towards them. I was lucky in that the last 5 years of my career I was able to accumulate most of the discretionary monies needed to reach my financial goals. Typically, it takes luck or many years to be able to retire early. I was probably more lucky than most.

It is also important to remember that you cannot continue to put off the planning for your retirement and try to "catch up" in the later years. When I was in my mid to late 40's, I established some goals that would enable me to retire early if I desired to do so. I decided that I wanted to keep my primary home and purchase a home at the Jersey shore and be able to afford a comfortable life style. To do this, I concluded that I needed a certain amount of income each year after I retired. This level of income then determined how much I needed to have in savings, stocks, pension funds, etc., which would generate the annual income needed.

For the next five years, I measured my progress towards this goal to ensure that I had a realistic and achievable plan. This also helped me make choices along the way. Some of my peers at work drove very expensive cars, purchased boats, took expensive vacations and purchased homes which, in some cases, could be considered extravagant. When I was faced with these choices, I decided in some cases that it was more important to have $100,000 more towards my retirement goal than to have a 30-foot boat. I chose to drive a company car instead of purchasing that Mercedes or Porsche. You cannot go overboard with this thinking. You certainly need to reward yourself and your family with some niceties along the way, but it is also important to maintain a balance between spending in the present and saving for the future.

In some cases, I probably erred by not buying things that I would have enjoyed, but in the long run I believe I made the right choices in most instances.

HAVE YOU MADE ANY LIFESTYLE CHANGES SINCE YOU RETIRED?

No major significant changes. I guess that my wife and I were always very sensible regarding our expenses and life style. We occasionally went out to dinner but it was typically once every two months or so. We always purchased new, reliable, mid-range automobiles that were great transportation but did not impress anyone. We spent a lot of money on our children's education, but I consider that to be an investment just like stocks or savings accounts. We live in a decent size home but certainly not one that I could have afforded with my salary level.

My children told me that I typify the person who is defined in the book "The Millionaire Next Door". I always purchased my suits at JC Penney, never spending more that $200. This has been my lifestyle all along and I do not feel a need or desire to change now. This life style and planning has enabled me to do certain things now that I sacrificed along the way. Just before retiring, I purchased a new sports car, which

I now enjoy and have the time to drive. I started collecting Lionel trains and plan to build a train layout in the basement. I had trains when I was very young, but like most children in my age group, they were discarded when we no longer played with them. I have always been fond of toy trains and appreciate the fact that I now can devote some time to them.

HAVE YOU MADE ANY CHANGES IN OTHER AREAS?

I have made no significant changes in other areas. One thing that has become more important is planning how to use the funds we have accumulated in order to maximize our returns and minimize our tax liability while using these funds to support ourselves.

ADDITIONAL COMMENTS

While I have retired early and listed a number of things that I planned to do, it is important to remember that my wife played a significant role in my career and our ability to do what we did.

Now we get to spend more time together, but my wife's job has not changed significantly from before. She still does most of the tasks around the house that she did prior to my retirement, with the exception that I try to do little things that help (i.e., food shopping). I try to remember that she should be enjoying this time as much as I and that she should be doing different things now that she might not have had the time to do before. Without her, none of this would have been possible.

I have another friend who is a Baby Boomer. He has been retired for the past seven years. Rather than filling out the questionnaire, he felt more comfortable submitting to an extensive interview and sharing his experiences with me. His only caveat was that I did not mention his name in the book.

This anonymous source leaking retirement information will be designated the code name, Deep Pockets.

Deep Pockets felt that he could be more candid and forthright about his experiences if his name was not mentioned, but I suspect that if friends and associates were aware of his good fortune, no pun intended, he might be perceived differently and possibly considered to be akin to a lending institution by people who lack scruples and fall into the category of opportunists.

That being said, how did Deep Pockets acquire his wealth? The old fashioned way, he inherited it! (Refer back to the top ten strategies to attain early retirement). I think most of us would agree that acquiring a large sum of money is the preferred method to commence retirement. You don't need a lot of retirement planning skills, and most of the worry and stress associated with your financial future dissolves. On the other hand, receiving and managing a significant sum of money is not as simple and automatic as you would think. Look at the documented stories of lottery winners who not only squandered their fortune, but reduced their lives to misery when they cashed that winning ticket. The entertainment and sport worlds are filled with rags to riches to rags stories about famous people who squandered obscene amounts of money. Historically, prize fighters are in a class by themselves in this arena. The champion who retires with some percentage of his earnings is the exception and not the rule.

Deep Pockets was fortunate. He was unaware that a trust fund had been established for him by his grandparent. It was only after he was married, had started a family and established himself in his chosen career that he became aware of his new found wealth. I believe that if you are brought up grounded and with what I call middle class values by your parents, you will be better served to deal with both the fortune and misfortune that life will surely offer.

The new wealth gave Deep Pockets the opportunity to retire from his job. He had been traveling all over the world for twenty-five years and realized he had one last opportunity to spend quality time with his youngest son and maybe make up for some of the family events that he had missed due to the rigors of his job. He decided to take one year off from his career and test the retirement waters. Like most Baby Boomers contemplating retirement, he had no clue what the future would hold for him. (If only he had the opportunity to read this book, I am sure his journey would have been smoother.) His one year test drive of retirement quickly turned into seven years and he has no itch to become gainfully employed.

I focused my interview with Deep Pockets on the subject and circumstances surrounding his purchase of a second home in Florida. In a previous chapter, Your New Dream House, we talked about the process of selling your home and moving to a planned community. However, for many Baby Boomers contemplating retirement, a frequent debate is the decision to move permanently to a planned community or to remain or downsize your present home and purchase a second residence in a warm and sunny destination. Of course, you can choose a third option and have endless theoretical discussions on the subject, do nothing, and continue to freeze your booty every winter.

On this topic, Deep Pockets is somewhat of a Baby Boomer pioneer, at least in the social circles that I frequent. He has been retired for seven years and now has owned his second house for three years. He is presently looking to establish permanent residency status in Florida. The following are the highlights from our conversation.

I asked Deep Pockets why he decided to purchase a second home. He explained to me that after being retired for several years, the expense of traveling and taking vacations was getting out of hand. Why not purchase a home in a resort area that would offer the amenities that he had utilized on past vacations? He could have a place to beat the winter blues, hopefully see the property value appreciate over time, and take advantage of a lower cost of living.

WHY FLORIDA?

Deep Pockets is a detail-oriented person and did due diligence before he purchased his new home. He checked out homes in the Caribbean and Arizona as well as Florida. He ultimately ruled out the Caribbean because in the final analysis, he and his wife did not want to live outside the United States. He wasn't impressed with Arizona's lunar landscape and said the only time he found green vegetation in the state, it poked him and made him bleed.

Living on the east coast, Florida was closer to family and friends than the other locations. Deep Pockets explained that Florida really can be divided into eight different sections, each with its own climate and personality. If you drew a line across the state from Tampa to Vero Beach, you must live south of that line if you desire tropical temperatures. Florida has no state income tax, a lower cost of living than up north, and favorable tax rates that extend to inheritance taxes. Or as Deep Pockets put it, "Florida is not only a good place to live, but it is also a good place to die."

DID YOU HAVE ANY PRE-CONCEIVED NOTIONS ABOUT FLORIDA PRIOR TO YOUR HOUSE SEARCH?

Deep Pockets and his wife had the standard concerns

that most potential residents of Florida share. Would my new friends and neighbors be the same age as my parents? Would a special night out mean playing multiple bingo cards at the Senior Center? Are portable oxygen tanks a medical necessity or merely a local fashion accessory?

WHERE AND WHY DID YOUR PURCHASE YOUR HOME?

Deep Pockets purchased a home in Palm City, Florida, just off of Route 95 and north of Jupiter. The community offered him the amenities he was looking for. The city is located on a river, which makes boating simple. The development has its own golf course, which is private, but managed by an outside concern. The cost of the golf membership and the golf fees are very reasonable, and with a third party running the club, you don't have to worry about the potential bickering of elitist members, or being hit with an expensive assessment fee. The community is not age restricted, but most of the residents are between the ages of fifty-five to sixty-five years old.

WHAT HAD BEEN YOUR BIGGEST SURPRISE SO FAR?

"On the plus side, my neighbors in the community are active, energetic, social animals. In general, most of the people I meet are interesting, successful people who retired fairly early in life and are committed to having a good time. My wife and I anticipated a quiet, laid-back lifestyle, instead it almost borders on hectic. On the other hand, while not a surprise, the reality of spending the summer months in this location in Florida is not pretty. It is always hot and humid and the weather pattern seemingly doesn't change. At times, during July and August, I thought I was Bill Murray in the movie, *GroundHog Day*."

Deep Pockets told me that you must educate yourself on Florida law and the state tax code and quickly secure the service of both a good accountant and attorney. He was stunned to see his property taxes increase thirty percent from the first year to the second year. A Florida resident (Deep Pockets is still classified as a New Jersey resident) has his yearly property tax increase capped at 3%. A home owner in Florida who is not a resident can have his taxes increased at the whim of the local government. Worse yet, for the non-resident Florida homeowner, this tax sword hanging over your head is transferable to the person who purchases your home, thus making the selling of your house less financially attractive.

To be considered a resident of the state of Florida, you must be living there for one hundred and eighty three days of the year. Not surprisingly, many states are not happy that they are now losing tax dollars from people who own multiple homes. Deep Pockets signaled out New York as being very aggressive in validating residency status. They will check phone records and other data to ensure that you are actually living less than six months in their state. Deep Pockets discovered that Florida has an intangible tax, which amounts to one percent of your assets, primarily directed at your stock and mutual fund holdings. This is a tax which can be circumvented legally with proper tax guidance. Yet, Deep Pockets was surprised how many people with no tax advice blindly filled out the form, and sent the government the full amount that was requested.

Deep Pockets assumed correctly that his Florida automobile insurance will decrease significantly. He didn't realize that his boat insurance will double when he becomes an official Florida resident. Even converting your New Jersey Blue Cross Blue Shield plan to Florida Blue Cross Blue Shield is not an automatic procedure. Deep Pockets has an existing medical condition. His Florida health insurance agent told him that Florida Blue Cross Blue Shield is not mandated and would not continue his health coverage in Florida. He currently is negotiating with additional health care providers for coverage. If he is successful, I am sure his premiums will be high and his coverage will be less than desirable.

I asked Deep Pockets how purchasing a second home impacted on family and friends. He said one of the keys for choosing a house was that it had to be appealing for his grown children and future grandchildren to vacation there. The warm weather, golf, tennis, swimming and boating make his house the perfect vacation retreat for his visiting children, and when they compute the cost of the vacation, which is free, mom and dad's home looks like a Trump resort. For similar reasons, friends and extended family have flocked to the new home. Deep Pockets appreciated all the company, but he could identify with proverb, "Family and friends are like fish. After three days they begin to stink."

I asked Deep Pockets if he thought he would eventually sell his home in New Jersey and move to Florida permanently. His answer was absolutely not. He did not want to abandon his New Jersey roots. However, he is looking to sell his present home and move into one of the adult communities starting to spring up in New Jersey. By downsizing and modernizing, he is looking to replicate the lifestyle he enjoys in Florida.

I asked Deep Pockets if he had any additional advice for Baby Boomers considering purchasing a home in Florida. He said make sure that you and your wife are in unanimous agreement about making the move. Don't take anyone's advice at face value. Do your own homework and research. Florida has been attracting retirees forever, and they are bracing for the migration of the Baby Boomer generation. Based on supply and demand, it is logical to conclude that real estate in Florida will continue to appreciate. If it is economically feasible, it is in your best interest to start the process sooner rather than later. Above all, keep a copy of *Has Anyone Seen My Reading Glasses?* close at hand to guide you through these unchartered waters. (He really didn't say this, but he might have, possibly when I wasn't around.)

CHAPTER 14
Retirement Adventures

One thing that I have done in retirement, but probably would not have done otherwise, is go skydiving. Before you get impressed, I am not talking about taking multiple lessons, and then jumping out of an airplane solo, relying on your own skill and ability. I am referring to Tandem jumping, a relatively new method of skydiving. The primary difference is that you are harnessed or tethered to the instructor. He makes most of the decisions and with minimum instruction, about two hours, you are ready to jump out of a plane at 13,000 ft. For some insane reason, I always wanted to jump out of a plane. This is contrary to my normal persona. I don't like heights. I am claustrophobic, and recently chickened out at the last minute standing on the line to enter Epcot's new Mission Space Ride.

Once I retired, I figured I had nothing to lose by jumping out of a plane. I had the time and the money. If I got hurt or was injured, I wasn't receiving a paycheck anyway. I had recently renewed my life-insurance policy. The timing was right. My two younger children had just recently graduated from college. To celebrate this notable achievement that they had completed an academic milestone, and more importantly, that I made my final tuition payments, we decided to take the big family vacation, spending one week in Las Vegas and one week in San Diego. I went on the Internet and planned our itinerary, searching for things to do in Las Vegas. I stumbled upon a skydiving facility located about half an hour outside the city. I read their promotional blurb, jotted down pertinent information, and made the decision to go for it. I told my three children what I had planned, and invited them to participate. To my surprise, my two sons declined. Their response was, "Are you crazy? You're not serious? Mom is going to kill you!" My daughter completely floored me, when she quickly said, "That sounds cool, Dad. I was hoping to go skydiving at some point in the future. It really sounds like fun."

We were in unanimous agreement on one thing, if Mom found out that Karin and I were going skydiving, this would be the worst vacation in family history. My wife's fear of flying rivals that of Mr. T. from the television series *The A-Team*. The few times she has flown on a plane she practically had to be drugged to calm her down. You combine this fear, with an abnormally strong maternal instinct, and you have a combination of Mr. T. and Harriet Nelson. I did not want to lie to my wife, but the haunting vision of her shackled to the plane on the runway screaming, "Hell, no, you will not go!" kept replaying in my mind. If I came clean with my wife and decided to make the jump with my daughter, she would become physically ill and the vacation would be ruined. If I bowed to her protests and didn't jump, I would feel resentful that I was denied an opportunity to fulfill a fantasy. The solution was obvious. I not only had to lie, but I had to include my children in a clever charade, that would keep my wife from knowing the truth.

I contacted a skydiving school and made the appointment for Karin and me. I kept Chris and Jay informed of my plans and what their roles would be in this ruse. The night before the jump, I spoke to my wife and explained to her that I wanted to spend some bonding time with Karin. I was playing a lot of golf with the boys and felt that I was neglecting Karin. Ethel volunteered to accompany us, but I insisted I needed a father/daughter day. I would take the car and be back early in the afternoon. The boys, chimed in on cue, "Hey, Mom. Let's have a bonding day of our own; we will jump in a taxi and check out some of the attractions. We need a break from Dad anyway." Ethel asked me where we were going to go. I told her I wasn't sure. The venue wasn't important, spending one-on-one time with Karin was the key thing. There was a lot of truth in what I had just conveyed to my wife. I wasn't lying. I just wasn't volunteering the whole truth. I went to bed trying to rationalize my actions, but unfortunately, I came to the realization that I possessed the same dubious skills of most politicians, certain CEO's, and just about every lawyer.

The next morning, Karin and I awoke early to leave for our appointment. I reminded her that the school alerted me to the fact that new skydivers have been known to lose control of their bodily functions, and did she pack an extra set of clothes? "Oh, yea," she replied. "I'm more concerned about that, than about jumping out of the plane. What about you?" "Are you kidding, this is your dad you're talking to," I responded, never admitting that I had packed an overnight bag and stuffed it into the trunk the night before. We arrived at the school and, surprisingly, neither one of us was nervous. We watched as the skydivers tumbled down to the earth, some more gracefully than others, but no major injuries or fatalities occurred. We pressed on.

The first thing we had to do was fill out paperwork. The paperwork was basically an intricate and lengthy document that held the skydiving school and its affiliates harmless for any possible circumstance that could occur while you were on their property. As I was browsing through the information, I looked up and saw a sign that said the entire process was being videotaped. After examining it further, I was sure the packet must have been authored by famous attorney, Johnnie Cochran, and he probably was watching the proceedings and having a good chuckle. I have been in the business world all of my adult life, and I had never seen such a lopsided document. I assured my daughter that the paperwork was a mere formality. They were trying to protect themselves from lawsuits, and based on the level of risk of their business, their insurance premiums must be through the roof. Karin seemed unconcerned. The questionnaire went something like this. "You are aware that skydiving is a dangerous sport. You can get seriously injured or die. If you get injured or die, it is not our fault. Check here to waive your rights. No one can guarantee that the equipment is 100% safe. (Hey, things happen.) If you get seriously injured or die, it's not our fault. Check here to waive your rights. The instructor you are skydiving with can make a mistake. (Who hasn't screwed up once in awhile?). If he causes your death or injury, it's not our fault. Check here. If you are seriously injured or die, you cannot sue us for any reason. Check here. If you are seriously injured or die, and think your heirs or beneficiaries of going to sue us, forget it. Check here." Every so often, they remind you that if you feel uncomfortable with signing your life away, no harm, no foul, your money will be cheerfully refunded.

My knees were starting to buckle, but what I didn't realize, was that the scary part of the process was coming up next. The instructor put a tape into the VCR. Karin and I filled out paperwork, according to the instructions. By the time I had signed the release, I was quite sure that if the school wanted to drop me out of the plane sans parachute, they were within their rights and could sue my survivors for the cost of the cleanup. At the end of the tape, they introduce you to the inventor of the Tandem Parachute—the man in whom I am putting my faith to make sure that my daughter and I arrived back to Earth safely. The inventor looks like Santa Claus strung out on drugs. He is speaking in German. The tape utilizes English subtitles to translate his message. The school has succeeded—now I am scared. I look around the hangar and notice the people who are going to jump today. Nobody is older than 25 and a significant number of skydivers are Japanese. The instructor converses with the students in Japanese. I am impressed. I'm not sure about the equipment, but the instructor seems to be sharp.

It is now time for our class to get instruction. We walk to the back of the hangar, where a mock plane has been built. They show you how to jump out of the plane and get into the banana position once you are freefalling, and how to land, among other things. I quickly became the poorest student in our group, repeating procedures two and three times to learn it properly. The last piece of instruction involved mimicking the proper body position in the plane, five minutes prior to the jump. We were told to get on our knees and then bend backwards so that our backsides were supported over our heels. The class had no problem. I thought I was doing fine when the instructor came over to me and asked why I wasn't in the proper position? "I thought I was," I responded. He then gently pressed his hand on my chest and pushed me backwards. I thought the quadriceps muscles in my legs we're going to pop. "I'm sorry," I said, "I'm not flexible. I can't go back any further." The instructor looked at me. "I strongly recommend that you cancel your jump. We will refund your money. You'll have to be on the plane for five minutes in this position. The chances are great that if you are that inflexible, your legs will cramp up prior to your jump. Once the plane is in the jump zone, we cannot return to the hangar. It would be unfair to the other students." I shot back at the instructor, "I've been here all morning waiting to jump out of a plane. I can take five minutes of discomfort. I am jumping." "Okay, then," shouts the instructor to the group. "Follow me, out to the runway. Let's get started!"

To my surprise, the adrenaline rush, or panic attack, that I had anticipated did not sweep over me, as Karin and I prepared to board our outdated Cessna. When I entered the plane, I was surprised to see the large amounts of duct tape that adhered to the interior walls. Was this a bad sign, or normal procedure for these types of planes? I quickly gave the benefit of doubt to standard operating procedure, and sat down on the floor. The plane had only one seat for the pilot, and room for Karin and me, and our two instructors. Our mentors introduced themselves. One young man, who looked like he could play Tom Cruise's role in the movie *Top Gun*, volunteered to jump with Karin. My partner was an outgoing fellow, who was built like an NFL nose tackle. We climbed to the 13,000 ft. mark with no trouble. I was amazed that no feelings of claustrophobia had engulfed me as we sat cramped in the small plane.

At last we got the signal from the pilot to get into the "position." It was five minutes until go time. I got on my knees. My face rested by the instrument panel next to the pilot. My Jump Master took his position, mounting me from behind. I turned to him and quipped, "Usually my date buys me dinner or at least a drink before I go this far." We had a quick laugh, and then he bent me backwards, putting me in the proper position as the instructor had done in the practice section. I was in immediate pain, but my problems were just starting. In no more than 30 seconds, my legs began to cramp up. It seemed every muscle below my waist was on fire. I couldn't move an inch. The Tandem Master asked me if I was cramping. He told me to hang on. In a few minutes, we would be jumping, and the pain would disappear.

Unfortunately for me, the tower would not give us permission to jump. It took us an additional twelve minutes of circling before permission was granted. The instructors, upon seeing my eyes filled with water and observing my head banging on the instrument panel, offered to abort the flight. I thanked them for the gesture, but I declined. The one benefit to this very bad situation was that I never had second thoughts about jumping out of the plane. The last couple of minutes prior to the jump were extremely painful. I gave serious thought to opening the door and leaping out. I really didn't care if the parachute opened or not, or if the instructor was coming along for the ride. Eliminating the pain was my only concern.

At long last, it was jump time. The door flew open and I couldn't wait to jump out of the plane. Unfortunately, my body was so badly contorted; I couldn't find the little gangplank outside the plane, which was the jump off point. My partner sarcastically commented. "You can't jump from inside the plane. You have to step on to the plank." Finally, I found the plank and jumped, without hesitation. As advertised, my cramps dissolved immediately.

Ironically, when you jump out of a plane, there is no feeling of plummeting to Earth. You feel like you're floating on a cushion of air. I was enjoying the scenery below, when my instructor started tapping my shoulder. Since you have the feeling of weightlessness, I actually forgot that I was attached to someone else. He kept tapping my shoulder, which was starting to annoy me. I thought, hey, I went through a lot to get here, leave me alone and let me enjoy the trip. The instructor started screaming at me, which at that altitude sounded like a whisper.—"Banana, banana." Duh! Once again, I had forgotten my instructions. You must get into the banana position, horizontal, with your back arched and your arms and legs extended, to sky dive properly; which was unlike the position I adapted, the straight plummet, also known as watch out below!

I was soon back on track and resuming my sightseeing of Lake Mead and the surrounding area. 30 seconds later without warning, my walk on Walden's Pond came to an abrupt end. The Instructor pulled the ripcord, and we catapulted skyward, as if we were shot out of a cannon. This must have been covered in our class, but somehow it hadn't registered with me. My flight suit had various cords attaching me to my Jump Master. The violent takeoff forced the belts to slip and attack my crotch, squeezing my genitals. Once we started to float down, the instructor asked. "How are you doing?" In my new Frankie Valli voice, I replied, "Fine." The ride down and the landing went as planned and were uneventful. The mission was accomplished! I met Karin in the hangar. She told me that her jump went off without a hitch. I related to her the rest of my story and she just laughed and was not at all surprised.

On the way back to the hotel room, I told Karin, "It's time to tell Mom the truth and confess. This could get ugly. If I start bleeding badly don't hesitate to call 911." I was only half kidding. My wife greeted me at the hotel. "Where have you been? You were gone all day and you didn't even call." "Honey," I sheepishly replied. "I have to be honest with you. Karin and I jumped out of a plane today." "Pat, be serious." she countered. I proceeded to tell her the day's events. She listened, and when I was done, she still thought I was pulling her leg. To validate my story, we had to walk back to my car, where

I pulled out the credit card receipt. I'm anticipating that my wife will speak to me again in late 2005 or early 2006.

Not all my experiences in retirement have been as intoxicating as jumping out of an airplane. Sometimes the most mundane of tasks can become fodder for a good story. When I was working for a living, I took great pride in the fact that I never went food shopping, nor for that matter did any domestic chores. I took the position that as the sole bread winner for the family I was the equivalent of the warrior in an Indian tribe. It was my mission to put the food in the teepee. Once I had bagged the game, my work was over and the squaw would cook the meal and take care of the clean up. For some reason, my wife did not share my tribal philosophy, but accepted the fact that I was a hopeless case, and that if she sent me shopping, I would probably create more aggravation for her.

I reconfirmed her fears, when years ago she gave me a list of things to buy at the Home Depot in town. I reluctantly accepted because she was feeling a little under the weather. Now, the Home Depot is a pretty big place and I was expecting to be thoroughly confused once I started shopping, but my problem was far more pathetic. I could not even find the building. After scouring the mall for 45 minutes, I gave up the hunt, ate lunch at a pizzeria, and returned home empty handed. I explained to my wife what had just taken place. She starred at me in amazement. "Pat, you couldn't find Home Depot because you went to the wrong mall." From that time forward she never bothered to ask me to go shopping again. Who says there are no rewards for being inept?

Anyway, now I am retired. I have no job and my wife is working on a regular basis as a substitute teacher in the middle school. On a recent summer day, I called the person who services my swimming pool and explained to him that the pool was starting to look like pea soup. He directed me to check the PH of the water. The PH was way too low. He suggested that I purchase about 25 pounds of baking soda. The baking soda is inexpensive. It will solve my problem and save me the cost of a service call. I thanked him for his input and took off for the local ShopRite. I pulled into the parking lot and almost immediately realized I was way out of my element. Women of all ages were steering their shopping carts in every direction. Cars were backing out of parking spaces, narrowly missing pedestrians who were engaged in conversation, and oblivious to their whereabouts. I felt like a visitor entering a foreign country who doesn't speak the language.

I quickly spied the many shopping carts parked in front of the entrance. They were jammed together in a shiny metal formation. I proceeded to yank a cart away, but the cart didn't budge. I pulled harder, but again achieved similar results. I started to feel foolish, but I kept my cool. I glanced at my watch, moved over to the side and waited for the next woman to try her luck at dislodging the cart. I observed the shopper putting a coin into a slot perched on the cart, and viola! the cart was disengaged, and off she went. Once she disappeared into the store, I quickly went back to free up a cart. I felt around my pants pocket for a quarter, but all I had in change was a dime and a nickel. I returned back to my car to see if I had a quarter buried somewhere, but of course I didn't. I pulled out the cash in my pocket and the smallest bill I had was a $5 bill. I knew the chances of someone in the parking lot giving me 4 singles and 4 quarters in exchange for my $5 bill was remote. Thus, I was forced to get in my car, leave the parking lot, and go to a gas station to get the necessary change. I returned to the ShopRite, deposited my coin, and entered this giant labyrinth they call a supermarket.

I had no clue where to start my Holy Grail-like journey for the baking soda, but like most members of my gender I found it distasteful to ask for directions. I asked myself which aisle the baking soda would be located. Baking soda can be used to clean laundry, bake cakes, be an additive for toothpaste, and evidently help clean your swimming pool. This product could be anywhere! I started my search at the logical place, aisle one, and proceeded to walk up and down the rows until I reached the end of the store. I did not find any baking soda and proceeded to reverse my journey from the last aisle to the first. Still no baking soda was discovered. By this time, I was not only angry I was also exhausted. If I were going to run a marathon, the ShopRite would not be my first choice as a training center.

This exercise had gone far enough. I flagged down the first ShopRite employee that I saw and asked her where I might find baking soda. She pondered for a few moments and then said she was not sure and would check with her supervisor. She came back 5 minutes later and directed me to aisle 4. I walked down the aisle, and just like my last two trips, I couldn't find the baking soda. Finally, another shopper took pity on me. I must have looked to her like Dustin Hoffman in the movie *Rain Man*. She practically took me by the hand and led me to my lost treasure, the baking soda. Of course, I had walked by this spot on three different occasions and failed to find what I was looking for. I thought to myself, "This is not my fault. The baking soda is on the bottom shelf, which was not in my primary field of vision and there were only 10 boxes left in the whole store. Doesn't management realize the endless ways that baking soda has been utilized for the benefit of mankind?" Before I could complete my rationalization, I remembered the many times I had "lost" my wallet or car keys. My wife would ask me if I had checked the car. "Of course, dear," I would reply in an irritated voice. "Obviously, that's the first place I checked." She would then go to my car and appear minutes later with my lost item. "All right, Pat, let's face it, you are just helpless." I muttered to myself, "Let's get out of this giant food maze and go home."

I proceeded to the checkout area and was surprised to see many of the shoppers running their credit cards though a terminal without any interaction from the cashier. My initial thought was, "Wow, technology at work in the supermarket!" I was half expecting that the purchased goods would be bagged automatically and a computer driven shopping cart would find its own way back to my car. The cashier awakened me from my science fiction fantasy with the words, "Paper or plastic?" I thought, "What is this, supermarket lingo? Doesn't anybody speak English anymore?" I said, "Look, lady, I have credit cards, but I prefer to pay in cash." The women behind me on line all started to laugh. The young clerk was doing all she could to prevent herself from "losing it." I knew I had made a faux pas, but didn't have a clue what it was. The cashier looked straight down at her feet. I suspect that if she made eye contact with me she would laugh in my face. "Sorry, Sir. Do you want the groceries bagged in a paper bag or a plastic bag?" "Are you kidding me," I mumbled. "Who cares? I have 6 boxes of baking soda; I don't even need a bag." I scooped up the baking soda, put the boxes in the cart and headed for the exit sign. The sun was shining directly into the store. I thought to myself,—"Follow the light, freedom is on the other side of the automatic door."

The door swung open and my escape was complete. I put the baking soda in the car and returned the cart to its rightful place. Then, I remembered I had deposited a quarter in the cart. The sign said you get your quarter back when you return the cart. I gently nudged the cart into another cart—no quarter. I tried excessive force and rear ended the cart in front of me—no quarter. This had been a long day and I was at the end of my rope. I treated the cart like a vending machine that swallows your money, but doesn't produce the can of soda you paid for. I kicked it, I beat it, I tried to choke the living quarter out of its hole, yet the cart seemed to mock me and refused to give in to my strong arm tactics. Finally, I was given a reprieve. A woman, observing my wrestling match and realizing that I was a rookie in the National Shopping League came to my rescue. She explained that my frustration was not my own doing; sometimes the mechanism gets jammed or broken. She handed me a quarter, took the cart off my hands and sped away.

As I drove home, I pondered all that had taken place during my maiden voyage to the supermarket. Most people probably would have wanted to return to the supermarket as quickly as possible to vanquish their demons. My initial thought was, "Food shopping, it's overrated. I could do it, but why?"

Another unique experience for me was the whole process of creating a book. I can tell you with absolute certainty that writing this book would never have been possible if I were still working for a living. The genesis for this project actually started in my youth, but I did not realize it at the time. In my case, when I was a boy, my parents took me to see several Broadway comedies. Often I was surprised how easily the audience laughed, even if the dialogue was, in my opinion, not all that funny. I'm not sure why this occurred. Maybe I had set artificially high standards for comedy because real life offers so many opportunities to squeeze out a good laugh. Did many theatergoers live in such a humorless environment that any comedy was welcome relief? Possibly, the realization that you paid a lot of money for the tickets motivated you to laugh easily to confirm that you had made a wise investment. Whatever the reason, I believed then and I believe today, that I could write a successful Broadway play. When my wife and friends would call me on this boast, my answer was always the same, "If I had the time, and didn't have to work for a living, I would be a successful playwright." I had this convenient cop-out for many years until I retired. Now my wife challenged me to put up or shut up. I was out of excuses and flying without a parachute. (See last chapter.)

It became crystal-clear that talking about doing something, and doing something, are two totally different things. Writing a play would not only take a lot of work, but additionally, I didn't even have a clue how to write a play. As a matter of fact, I had not really written anything. My lifetime body of work included reviews of timeshare resorts that I had visited, a letter to a judge haranguing the judicial system for ruling against my mother in a medical malpractice case, and my son's essay on his college application form which covered the topic of a Person I Most Admired. I volunteered myself to be the subject of this composition, and since I had first hand knowledge about the subject matter, it was easy to wax eloquently about the mythical attributes this person possessed. I was having too much fun in retirement to write a play. Travel, sports, etc., were taking too much of a toll. Where would I find the time? If I got bored or ran out of things to do, I would start a major literary project.

There is no doubt in my mind that had the stock market not plummeted, this book would never have been written.

As a longtime sufferer of A.L.S. (Acute Laziness Syndrome), it would take a lot to motivate me to undertake such a vast project. My dwindling bank account and a stretch of rotten weather in New Jersey served as the catalyst to write my play. Then I remembered, I don't know how to write a play, and my attention turned to writing a book. Sure, I needed the money, but my ambitions were far loftier. Friends and neighbors looked up to me as a role model. "Look at that S.O.B. Pat. I'm going to work, and he is loading up his car to play golf. I can't wait to retire and become a goof-off like that guy." If I ended my reign of fun and went back to work, I would crush the dreams and stamp out hope for many of my peers. It was a heavy burden to bear, but I picked up the gauntlet. I researched a number of possible subjects to be the basis for my book. I quickly realized that I had virtually no legitimate expertise on any topic that would generate interest to the book-buying public. Then it hit me—I could write a book on retirement. After all, who has the ability to do nothing and do it well better than I? One night while the family was gathered at the dinner table, I proclaimed that I was going to write a book. Nobody reacted, and they continued with their meals.

For the first three months, I did a lot of planning, organizing, researching, and mostly talking about my new undertaking. Unfortunately, I did very little writing. It was far easier to talk about the book than write about the book. Nobody, including me, took this project seriously, but as a source for family entertainment, the book was a hot topic. Before one word was written, we had mock debates over which television shows I would make a guest appearance on. Is Katie and Matt the right venue to market my book? Should I get Oprah to champion my book? Who is going to play me in the movie? Should I maintain artistic control? Even though nobody expected me to finish the book, it was interesting to see how they hedged their bets. "Am I going to be in the book, and if so, are you going to portray me in a positive light?" "I don't know," I would reply, "but it might be in your best interest to treat me very nicely during the creative process, and the creative process can take a long time." Once I declared that I was writing a book, I had a built-in excuse to do even less around the house than usual (if that were humanly possible). When my wife wanted me to do domestic chores or take her shopping, I would invoke my author's prerogative: "I would love to help out, Honey, but I have a few ideas that just came to me that I need to jot down on paper." One never knows when the creative juices will flow!

After three months, my written output for the book consisted of one page, a rough draft for the introduction. My children spotted the work on my desk, and they demanded that I read what I had accomplished so far. I declined, explaining that this was a crude outline. They persisted, claiming that after three months of me verbalizing about the book, they had earned the right to hear the first words of my epic novel. I relented and reluctantly read what I had put down on paper. Chris, Karin, and Jay bowed their heads and clenched their teeth in silence, as I continued with my oration. When I finished, Jay broke the uncomfortable silence. "Dad, I'm not saying this to bust your chops, but this stinks! You are wasting your time. You'll never finish one chapter of this book; go back to work and get a real job." Everyone at the table started to laugh. I realized that my son was right. I had to either stop play-acting at writing a book, or really take this project seriously. That night my quest to be an author commenced.

I made an important step forward in the writing process in Puerto Vallarta, Mexico. I was there with friends of ours, on a timesharing vacation exchange. The resort, a beautiful oceanfront property, did their usual full-court press to entice us to meet with their sales team. The other couple, unfortunately, was actually interested in knowing more about the new facilities and timesharing opportunities at the resort. We met with a salesperson the following day, prepared and experienced in what the next two hours would be like.

At this point, I had written about 10% of the book. Rodney Dangerfield had gotten more respect than I was getting from family and friends. The salesperson started the Inquisition with my friend Ken, asking him all the basic boilerplate questions. She then turned her attention to me, and repeated the standard questionnaire. She queried, "Occupation?" I fired back immediately, "Writer." My wife, Ken, and Linda started to go into convulsions of laughter. I remained motionless. The salesperson tried to remain professional and continued to ask me questions. "A writer, really! Have you written anything that I might be familiar with?" "I don't think so. I've written reviews in the past, and I am in the process of writing a book. Presently, I am unpublished," I said, rather matter-of-factly. My wife and friends exploded into another round of laughter.

We were now officially making a scene. The other marketing presentation groups surrounding us were now completely distracted and staring in our direction. Our salesperson, a very accomplished veteran in the time-share game, finally broke down. "OK, what's going on here? Let me in on the joke." I calmly apologized for the behavior of the others, and gave the flustered salesperson a brief explanation, and informed her that my threesome didn't feel that "writer" was warranted as my present occupation. The salesperson seemed relieved, as the joke was not on her, and more importantly, the cause of our outlandish behavior didn't disqualify us from buying a timeshare week. She pressed on with her sales pitch and eventually the meeting ended without a purchase.

This little stunt, besides providing amusement for my wife and friends, did actually serve as a source of motivation for me. I liked the moniker, "Pat Paciello, Writer." If I were a writer and thus employed, I might be able to qualify for the free set of golf clubs that they were giving away to tour the resort community in Pennsylvania. Seriously, the journey for the first time became more important than the destination. Sylvester Stallone, on the eve of his first fight with Apollo Creed in *Rocky* didn't ask to win the fight; he just wanted to be standing when the final bell rang. If I could complete this book, I would gain a tremendous sense of personal accomplishment, which just might be the final piece of the puzzle to make retirement as satisfying as possible.

Writing a book offers a whole set of challenges, but actually going from the writing stage to seeing a book published in some way shape or form is a very interesting process. Since I had no experience in writing a book; I had even less of a clue as to how to make this happen. My friend Jane Cooper gave me my first insight into the marketing process. She was at the time writing a non-fiction book and had already contracted with an agent from a prestigious New York literary firm to represent her. Jane gave me an overview of the entire publishing process, explained to me the value of having an agent, and offered to give me an introduction to her agent.

By this time, I had written about one third of the book. The idea that I would be talking to some hot shot agent about my manuscript was both amusing and intimidating. As I prepared for the call, I felt like I did when I interviewed for my first job after graduating college. I couldn't believe that I was actually nervous. I called the agent numerous times over the course of the week and received no call back. I was by this time developing an excellent rapport with his secretary, and thanks to her she practically forced the agent to talk to me.

The agent was very smooth and laid-back in his approach. He started to ask me the obvious questions about my manuscript which I handled flawlessly. Then he switched gears and said, "Pat I have to ask you a number of questions that perspective publishers are going to ask of me, and your answers will help me gauge whether your manuscript will be appealing to them. He then gave me an overview of how the publishing industry works and why it is so difficult for a new writer to get his book published today. Now that I was depressed, he asked me, "Have you ever written any other books on retirement?" It was difficult for me not to laugh out loud. Obviously, he had no concept of whom he was talking to. I queried him back. "Do you mean books targeted for the retirement community?" "Yes," he replied. "Well, this is my first project on the subject," I responded. (I tried to sound like I had written books on other subjects, and hoped he wouldn't follow up and ask me what other books I had written.) He didn't. He asked me if I was actively involved in a leadership capacity with any retirement organizations? Did I give seminars to large groups on the subject? Could I produce press clippings and newspaper articles demonstrating my expertise on the subject matter?

I felt like David battling Goliath without a slingshot. I answered him the way politicians respond when they want to sidestep a difficult question. "I believe what you are really trying to determine is whether I have the expertise, contacts, and motivation to market this book? The answer is absolutely! I have almost thirty years experience in the business world, all in a marketing and managerial capacity. I am comfortable making presentations in front of large groups of people, and not only relish the opportunity to market this project, but I have the time to do so." I was on a roll now, and was tired of being in a defensive   posture.

I quickly followed up my comments with a question to the agent. In a slightly pompous tone I asked, "I know you're representing Jane on her manuscript, but mine is quite different. My book takes on a serious subject, but humor is the real common denominator which makes it unique. Have you ever represented an author in this type of genre before?" The agent made a bigger transformation than David Banner turning into the Hulk. He was now trying to convince me that he possessed the experience and know-how, to represent my book. He recited to me his resume covering all the various projects that he has represented. I tried to politely interrupt him, to let him know that I was impressed with his credentials, but he was bound and determined to finish his monologue. The conversation ended and I agreed to send him my partially written manuscript. I never heard from him again.

My next adventure, in the "How do I get my book published saga," came courtesy of Larry McMillian. Larry has written several successful business books and is considered the guru of options trading. (I guess you could say that he wrote the book on the subject.) He was kind enough to refer me to a publishing company which had represented several of his books. I went on the firm's website and saw that they were a niche publishing firm primarily specializing in high level business books. My partially written manuscript could have been compared with *Fun With Dick and Jane*, while their inventory of books that they published were more closely linked with *How to Build a Nuclear Bomb at Home for Fun and Profit*. I saw absolutely no connection with the publishing firm, but I was greatly appreciative and excited that I was going to have an audience with them. I was in effect skipping the agent part of the process and going straight to the decision maker. (We don't need no stinking agents.)

To my shock and amazement, the publishing company treated me like I was the reincarnation of Ernest Hemingway. They could not have been nicer or more professional. I thought Larry must be quite valuable to the company, considering the way they are rolling out the red carpet for me. I passed this on to Larry who offered an additional reason for the firm's attentiveness. It seems that Larry had recently referred to them a friend who had written a book that was in their wheelhouse for subject matter. The publishing firm hemmed and hawed about representing the book and eventually the writer sold his book to a rival firm. The book was a money maker and the publishing firm kicked themselves for letting a golden opportunity slip through their fingers. Larry then refers me to the firm and they are not about to make the same mistake twice.

I'm a realist and I told the publishers that I couldn't imagine, if they wanted the book, how it could be a good fit for them. They said I may be right, but they wanted to make that decision. During the next six weeks I submitted what I had written. They gave me critical feedback coupled with positive reinforcement. I submitted at their request, additional chapters that they reviewed carefully. Finally, my work went before their editorial committee, where an offer or rejection of the manuscript would be the final outcome. I had to laugh when I imagined what that final meeting must have been like. A group of seasoned editors surrounding a conference table evaluating high brow business books, then suddenly my contact blurts out *"Has Anyone Seen My Reading Glasses?* is our next manuscript."* After her presentation, did the savvy veteran editors stone her, or did they think that someone was playing a practical joke on them? Maybe they were amazed that my book had actually gone this far into the process. I will never know, but the committee concurred with my original assessment and passed on the book.

I was far from discouraged. In a short period of time, I had made contact with both an agent and a publishing company. I continued to write while sending out query letters and book proposals to agents and book publishers. I checked my e-mail frequently. When I did get a reply to my inquiry, it was always a rejection, but it was formatted in the most sensitive way. It evoked those feelings you had in high school, when you had the hots for some girl, but she told you that she just wanted to be friends. Even though the traditional trail to publishing had gone cold, I was investigating self-publishing and print-on-demand alternatives. Most importantly a new golf season had just begun and my attention drifted from writing to how to lower my handicap.

After finishing a round of golf with my friends Al and Neil, we headed for lunch and a few cold ones at the Mount Olive Eatery, commonly known as Moe's. I was sitting at the bar when a young woman walked in and sat down next to me. (I know this sounds like the beginning of a joke that gets passed around the internet but it's not.) She and the barmaid or mixologist or what ever they call a bartender these days embraced and exchanged hugs. They obviously knew one another, and after they exchanged pleasantries, the bar maid poured the woman a drink which included four or five different liquors. I was watching the customer to gauge her reaction when she tasted this exotic concoction.

To my surprise, instead of drinking this potent potion, the woman pulled out a camera and started snapping pictures of the beverage from different angles. It reminded me of those supermodel photo ops that you see in magazines, like the *Sport's Illustrated* Swimsuit edition. I half expected the woman to say something to the glass like, "Work with me, baby, or "relax be yourself." The scene brought back memories of a Saturday Night Live show produced many years ago, when SNL was still very funny. They did a skit on Elvis's coat, treating the coat like the real Elvis, and breathing life and personality into an inanimate object.

Of course, as I am watching the lady photograph the drink, I think this spectacle is very funny and ask her for an explanation. She tells me she is a reporter and is doing a story on the drink of the week. I suggested to her, tongue in cheek, that maybe she should write the article from the drink's perspective. The drink could narrate a story describing the motley crew huddled around the bar each with a unique tale to tell, and confess what they were doing hanging out at a bar at two-thirty on a Thursday. Instead of calling me an idiot, she politely mentioned that she once wrote an article on dogs from the dog's point of view. I excused myself and went to the men's room; on my return I almost brushed against the magnificent drink. I apologized to the glass for invading its space.

I told Ellen, the reporter, that many years ago when I was in college at Fairleigh Dickinson a bartender at a local bar called the Elms made the very same drink. Back then it was called The Journey's End. It tasted sweet and went down smooth, but after two drinks you became comatose. She thought that was very interesting and asked if she could quote me in the paper. I thought, "How is this going to look, jobless man hangs out in bar during the week and recalls drinking stories from his youth." Having no shame, I replied, "Sure."

I asked her what paper she wrote for. I expected her to say one of the small newspapers published by a local town. My eyes opened when she said *The Daily Record*, a newspaper that serves the residents of Morris County and the paper that I have delivered to my home. Sensing an opportunity, I immediately launched into my "I'm writing a book" speech. I got about half way through my sales pitch when she politely interrupted me and said, "Your book sounds fantastic. Our paper is looking to feature an article on retired Baby Boomers and I am sure that they would love to include you in the article."

When she left Moe's, she handed me her business card and wrote her editor's name and phone number on the back. She told me that if I weren't contacted by the paper in a couple of days, then I should call the editor directly. Neil and I both looked at each other with the same open-mouthed facial expression that was common with Spanky and Alfalfa during *The Little Rascals* episodes. I said to Neil, "What a break. I could be getting some free publicity on a book that hasn't been written, by a writer that hasn't written anything else."

Two days later the drink of the week article appeared in the paper sans my input. "That's okay, I rationalized. "I can keep my dignity for a little while longer." Two more days pass and I have still not been contacted by the newspaper. I call the editor of *The Time of Your Life* magazine, an insert of *The Daily Record.* I get voicemail and leave a message that should get me a return phone call. "Hi, Carol, my name is Pat Paciello. I met your reporter, Ellen, in a bar and maybe she had one too many of the drinks of the week, but she thought that you would be interested in interviewing me for an article in your magazine. Please call me if you want to pursue this." I thought that I would surely get an immediate response, but none was forthcoming. Two more days passed and still no contact from the paper. I now assumed this interview was a dead issue or a hoax. Other than having a good story to share with family and friends, I was back to square one as far as getting publicity for the book was concerned.

The next day, I get a phone call from Navid Iqbal of the *Daily Record*. My first thought is why would he call me to subscribe to the paper when I already have it delivered on a daily basis? He gets my full attention when he tells me that he is a reporter and he would like to do a story on me. He asks if we could meet tomorrow because he wants to get the article in the paper for Saturday. Understanding my priorities, I decline because I have a tee time for the next day. He says "No problem. I can interview you at the golf course and bring a photographer to take pictures." I'm starting to get a little leery now. Am I going to be a victim of a Candid Camera episode or are my friends playing a practical joke on me? I agree to meet Navid at the headquarters of the Record after my round of golf is completed. He greets me in the reception area. He is a sharp, very professional reporter. We spend almost two hours together. He seems fascinated that a relatively young man is retired, basically enjoying life, and making no apologies. I, on the other hand, try to direct the interview to my book, hoping to garner some pre-publishing buzz. When the interview concludes, he asks me if he can call my wife later and interview her. I laugh and say, "Sure, good luck," knowing that my wife will be apprehensive in this interview format.

I returned home from the interview and told my wife and children what had transpired. As usual my children's support for me was unwavering. My son Jay said, "Dad, you being interviewed by anyone is indicative of how slow news is breaking in Morris County." I couldn't disagree with him. My daughter's response was, "You have got to be kidding me." My wife was all smiles until I told her that she would be getting interviewed soon. She reacted predictably. "What, you're not serious?" She asked me what kind of questions he would ask her, and how she should respond. I said, "Be honest as you always are and everything will be fine." Navid called later in the evening, and according to my wife, the interview went off without a hitch. As I lay in bed that night a disturbing thought hit me. What if Navid was doing an article on retired Baby Boomers, and he portrayed me as a lazy, shiftless person who was fortunate to have a devoted caring wife who allowed me to indulge in my leisure-time pursuits. Not only would this kill the book, but The National Organization of Women could mobilize and start picketing my house. I might become the Al Bundy of this decade! I quickly dismissed this notion. After all, Navid had spent considerable time with me and got to know my personality and philosophy on retirement. Then I really started to worry.

On Saturday morning I got dressed and headed up the driveway before 7:00 am. Since I had retired, I couldn't remember leaving the house this early and not playing golf. My plan was to read the article. If the story were positive, I could go back to sleep. If it were negative, I could go on a rescue mission and commandeer my neighbors' newspapers to avoid embarrassment.

I really had no idea if the article would even be printed. Maybe someone in the editorial department would come to his senses and ask the obvious question. "Why are we doing an article on this guy?" Sure enough, the article was in the *Time of Your Life* section of the newspaper. It covered two pages and included a big picture of a guy that looked a lot like me. More importantly, the article was well-written and featured and referenced the soon-to-be written book. My good fortune was not over yet. The next day, Sunday, in the magazine section, the paper mistakenly reprinted my story.

I would be lying if I said that I didn't enjoy my fifteen minutes of fame that the article brought me. I teased my wife and told her that I received three marriage proposals. Without hesitating she fired back, "I hope you accepted one of them." I did get a phone call from another reporter who was doing an article on early retirement. She interviewed me and a second story should be in the newspapers soon. All of a sudden, at least locally, I had become the sensei of early retirement.

I don't know how this chapter of retirement will end, but if you are reading this book, it means my journey to somehow publish it was successful. I can now check off one more thing that I have accomplished in retirement that wouldn't be possible if I were still working. Next up, running with the bulls in Pamplona, or preparing for Nathan's hot dog eating championship in New York City. Hmmmm, tough choice. Pass the mustard.